The Complicated Gray

THE COMPLICATED GRAY

A Big Story of
RESILIENT REDEMPTION

Justine Froelker

XULON PRESS

Xulon Press
2301 Lucien Way #415
Maitland, FL 32751
407.339.4217
www.xulonpress.com

Printed in the United States of America.

ISBN-13: 978-1-54565-045-5

Dedication

To the sad, broken, angry, too much, and not enough… may you fight your way to *and* receive His love.

the complicated gray

noun

1. the space that exists between two truths and the embodiment of both
   ex: the childless mother, the doubtful believer, etc.
2. the muck between, what we have been taught, are two opposing emotions and feeling them at the same time
   ex: happy *and* sad

synonym
the permission of The And

When we give ourselves permission to walk into the muck of the complicated gray and embrace the space of both joy and longing, anger and acceptance, happy and sad, giving ourselves permission to live with the permission of The And.

It is here that our clarity, healing, and magic lie.

Letter to the Reader

In your hands you hold the story of a mighty faith wrestle.

It is messy.

It will be difficult to read at times.

It will make you laugh and cringe.

Shudder and shake your head, both in a 'me too' and a 'I can't believe she wrote that' way.

It will make you yearn and swell.

I used to call my story hard, sad, and unlucky.

That is until I chose to make it a gift and see it is all how He led me to Him.

It is a big story of resilient redemption.

You see, I am a messy and imperfect Christian.

Aren't we all?

Isn't that exactly why we need Jesus?

So much of what is out there in the faith, and especially the religion realm, presents this façade of perfection. A picture that has made me question if I am Christian enough to write, speak, and work in ministry.

The thing is, God doesn't use the perfect or qualified. He chooses us, flaws and all. He loves us, flaws and all. He always chooses us.

All this to say, you will read curse words in this book.

Believe it or not, I have softened many of them quite a bit in hopes that my words are not a stumbling block to someone, especially to someone who really yearns for this downright scandalous love of Christ, whether you met Jesus long ago or haven't just.

The walk into His arm is not an easy journey for many.

Which I think is the very reason we all need the damn curse words...

Life is messy and people are complicated, and sometimes a blasphemous shit, and yes the occasional F-bomb, helps us to live, love, and lead with our faithful, whole heart more easily.

Is the Lord always working on me?

Yes.

Am I always a work in progress?

I'd hope we all are.

I suppose what I ask is that you don't allow one of the words I couldn't remove stop you from meeting my Jesus.

Keep reading, you will meet Him.

He will love you and change everything.

He has for me.

Justine

Prologue

I was sad. Now, I'm pissed...and when I'm pissed, I cry...and I'm tired of both.

The human and inherent need to be seen, to be known, and to be loved is the space for which we yearn, as if to be *at* and *in* our home both within ourselves and connected with others.

Yet, as a childless mother, I feel invisible, like I never fit in.

Almost everywhere I go, I am the only woman in her mid-thirties without children.

Where do I belong?

Can I ever belong?

How can I possibly belong?

I am a woman who wanted to be a mother, a woman who paid a lot of money and put my body (and my surrogate's body) through synthetic hormonal hell to become a mother.

I am a mother without my own children. And yet, I am a mother to many.

> *"Sing, barren woman,*
> *you who never bore a child;*
> *burst into song, shout for joy,*
> *you who were never in labor;*
> Isaiah 54:1

Chapter 1

"It's pretty obvious that we are the visitors."

"Which one is this?" Chad asked as he drove us through the city streets of Saint Louis.

"I don't know honestly…just one that was close and seemed like an option," I replied. We had been dating for about nine months and church shopping for at least six of those months, a journey that was proving to be nearly impossible for two people who grew up so differently.

"It's smaller than some of the other ones," he said as he grasped my hand and we walked through the chapel doors, wondering just what awaited us on the other side.

"Oh," we both muttered under our breath as we entered through the doorway. I looked up to make eye contact with him as we felt every parishioner turn to look at us.

"Too late to walk out now," he said with a smirk.

We took our seats in the middle pew, fully aware of the eyes following us. My heart began to pound harder and harder as I became more and more uncomfortable, not knowing what to expect at all from this particular church service besides (hopefully) some great music.

We clapped along with the congregation, and we sang. I mean, we 'sang', though neither one of us was quite comfortable enough to exclaim the occasional "Amen" out loud like most others in the congregation. After the pastor read some scripture, she said, "We would love all our visitors to stand so that we can welcome you."

"Do we really have to?" I asked, looking at Chad. "It's pretty obvious we are the visitors."

"I think so," he replied with that smirk right back on his face.

We stood together in a sea of the most welcoming, cheerful, and faithful people we had ever had the pleasure of meeting. Instantly, we were overwhelmed with handshakes, hugs, and yellow roses as most of the members left their seats to welcome us, two obviously new-to-the-church people who also happened to be the only two white people in this church on that beautiful Sunday morning.

After the greetings, the pastor continued her sermon with a beautiful message, one with which I identified and learned a ton. By hour two, the incongruous rumble of my stomach broke my concentration. Chad glanced at me and tried not to laugh. "We are so late for meeting my parents for brunch," he whispered.

"How much longer do you think this will go on?" I replied. "I am so hungry!"

At three hours, the fantastic service finally came to a close. As we headed toward the doors, several people approached us with a flurry of encouraging statements and invitations to return next Sunday.

"So good to see you!"

"We hope you enjoyed it!"

"Please come again!"

Then, a very warm and kind woman put her hands on my shoulders and said, "We are so glad you stuck it out, but we understand if you don't feel like this is your church home. Please know you are always welcome back."

"Thank you," I replied.

Walking back out to the car, we both began to laugh.

Once he had recovered from his fit of laughter, Chad looked at me and asked, "Did you know?"

"It's not like it said on a church's website who their demographic is!" I retorted a little sheepishly.

"We tried it, and I actually liked it," he replied with a grin.

"Me too! Would you want to come again?" I asked.

"Think they allow snacks?"

God – 0

Justine – 1

Haven't you ever kept score with God?

Whatever you heard me teach before an audience of witnesses, I want you to pass along to trustworthy people who have the ability to teach others too.
2 Timothy 2:2

Chapter 2

I can still be pissed and get my butt to church.

"I'm telling you. You have to try this church. I think it is exactly what you need," my officemate, friend, and fellow therapist Kelly J. said as we stood in our little office kitchen discussing the latest tale in *The Incredible Adventures of Justine and Chad Go Church Shopping*. Our God talk is typical in the office as we pass one another between clients, or while standing in the kitchen under the harsh fluorescent lighting we don't allow in our actual therapy offices and waiting room.

"You keep saying that," I replied with a slight eye roll.

"It has been awhile…you think you're ready?" she asked with compassion in her voice.

"I know I want to be," I replied.

"It's Christmas. Try it," she urged.

She's right. I can still be pissed and get my butt to church.

Between an infertility journey that ended without babies in our arms and a new pastor at the church we were calling home, it had been a while since Chad and I had attended a service. I knew we both wanted and needed to be there, and yet, I couldn't find the strength inside of me to praise a God who handed me a life without kids. Thankfully, Chad knew better than to push and never forced me to go when I just wasn't ready.

I looked up the service times over the next three days.

Good God! Eight services! Four left tomorrow night on Christmas Eve.

With a sigh, I decided we would go and check it out.

I texted Chad, "Can you be out of work in time to go to a Christmas Eve church service?"

"Yep," came the short replied.

Oh boy. Here we go again.

"Holy crap! It's like its own compound," I said as Chad turned on his signal to pull into the long drive flanked by a little airport on the left and a leveled cornfield on the right. The small road led up to a massive building that looked like it belonged in Colorado, not suburbia West unty, Saint Louis.

"It's huge!" I said as we walked into the biggest lobby I'd ever seen. The size of the structure was impressive, especially for a church. The walls were painted a series of warm, welcoming colors, and the beams made of beautiful untreated, dark mahogany wood. The sounds of chatter, laughter, and that bit of annoying Christmas joy filled every crevice. People were everywhere, and I could not stop myself from looking all around with a face of childlike wonder that must have gotten the volunteers' attention. As I made my way through in, one of the volunteers approached us with a huge smile and asked, "First time here?"

"Yes," I replied softly.

5

"Well, we are already in overflow seating. If you do come back, just so you know, for Christmas and Easter, it is always best to get here at least 30 minutes early if you want to sit in the auditorium."

I looked up at Chad with disappointment in my heart, "Okay," we both said in return.

"Follow me. I'll take you to The Loft, where you can watch the service."

God – 0

Justine – 2

You got me here, and I have to watch a screen?

How long, O Eternal One? How long will You forget me? Forever?
How long will You look the other way?
Psalm 13:1

Chapter 3

"I'd like to think He knows I needed more than this."

We sat in a dark room lined with chairs and a huge movie screen. My heart began to beat slightly faster as my breath caught and tears came to my eyes. Chad grabbed my hand and squeezed. He knew my body language, which meant that he also knew I must be wrestling. "You okay?" he asked quietly.

"This sucks. Seriously, how good can this be just watching it? I'd like to think He knows I needed more than this," I muttered, letting some of my frustration filter through into my words.

The lights went black, and the screen suddenly came to life with the band who began to play the most beautiful and amazing music I'd heard in a long time. After a few songs, the lights came up a bit just as a man with funky glasses and a head full of crazy cool hair walked on stage and said something along the lines of, "Hi everyone! Merry Christmas! I am your lead pastor, Greg. We are so happy you are here and hope you enjoy the service. I just wanted to stop in and said hello, thank you for coming, and wish you a Merry Christmas." The next thing I knew, he appeared on the screen to deliver His message…a message of Christmas hope on the cross, unlike anything I had ever heard. A message that apparently my heart was ready to receive after all this time finally.

The lights dimmed some, and he led the congregation in prayer. The lights changed again in the middle of the prayer as I realized tears were still in my eyes. The lights turned a third time as the music began to fill the room again. As the music ended and the lights came up, Chad grabbed my hand to get up and leave with everyone else, but my body needed to sit there for a bit longer.

I looked at him with tears in my eyes. "That was incredible," I said.

"It really was."

I took a breath, looked up, and let His warm embrace surround me.

God-1

Justine-2

He showed me, and damn it.

I will plant a new heart and new spirit inside of you. I will take out your stubborn, stony heart and give you a willing, tender heart of flesh.
Ezekiel 36:26

Chapter 4

"For a lot of people, it isn't that simple."

After that Christmas Eve service, we attended every weekend. The music, like the songs you hear on the radio, usually left me with tears rolling down my face. The message was applicable to our lives and simultaneously filled with biblical history. It was the perfect combination for Chad and me. We had finally found our church home.

Slowly, ever so slowly, the score I had been keeping with God started to head in His favor. I knew I would only be able to find couples like us, without kids, in a congregation like this; it had to be a huge one.

Surely, we couldn't be the only ones in this massive sea of people who did not have children of their own.

"We have a big church, but we can feel like a small one. Sign up for one of our classes and get started," one of the associate pastors declared during the announcements before Greg started the message for the week.

"You ready to try a class?" Chad asked as we headed to brunch after service.

"I think so. *Explorations* is probably where we should start," I said, already thinking about how delicious a blueberry scone sounded right then. Looking at the description of the class, I read it out loud to Chad.

"*Explorations* is the class the church offers as kind of an 'introduction to doctrine.' What does that even mean? It's a class you take to learn about other religions, scripture, and doctrine. It's where you find a Bible you love and learn about surrender, grace, and accepting Jesus as your Savior."

Here we freaking go.

"This better not be a freaking Bible study," I said to Chad as he drove us to our first *Explorations* class.

"Would that be so bad?" he asked as he tried and failed to hide a grin that said all too clearly what he thought about this class.

"I don't feel like I know enough of the Bible to do one. I've never even been in Sunday school or anything like that," I complained.

"I think that is kind of the point then," he quipped back.

We'd been attending this new and surprising, albeit "mega church" as my sister called it, for a few months now. We hardly ever missed a weekend.

Oddly enough, at this point, I loved church.

I was still pissed at God, and I loved church anyway.

"Any and all questions are welcome here," seems to be the tagline of the church–especially in the *Explorations* class.

I could feel my heart pound harder as Chad spotted his table and then mine. "I'm on this side. I'll see you in a couple of hours," he said before he took his seat.

Not only did I have to meet nine new people, I also had to explain that:

"No, we don't have kids. Yes, we tried. No, we're not adopting,"

And, I also had to confess my faith testimony. What would they said if I said, "Well, God lets crazy pants over there have all the babies she wants and I get none, so yep, I am pretty pissed at Him."

I noticed the cute woman with beautiful brown hair right away. She had a spunkiness to her wardrobe and an expression that I could identify with right away, so I sat next to her.

"I'm Justine," I said as I slid into the chair next to hers.

"Hi, I'm Laurie," she replied with a big smile.

The first class was basic introductions. I had been assigned to sit at a table with a strong believer, a few people who grew up Catholic, a couple of Christians, and then the two stricken women: me and my new friend, Laurie. This was going to be an interesting first class.

All these believers got to sit with the woman who can't have kids and the one whose husband died of cancer a year prior, lucky them!

"My husband's memorial was in this room," Laurie told the table when telling us a bit about her story.

My eyes immediately filled with tears. Her grief was palpable and was becoming synergistic with mine.

All in the house of God.

Comforted? Some.

Pissed? Yep.

Confused? Definitely.

What are You doing? I wondered as I glanced up at the ceiling and then back down to the woman next to me.

What are you planning for me now?

The question holding me back every class is: WHY?

Why give me the babies and then take them away?

Why no actual babies?

Why would He have me go through the journey of even trying?

Why would He hurt so many people in the process of losing this dream?

I suppose it all boils down to one real question: *Why do bad things happen to good people?*

This is the question that plagues every single person who wants to believe in a loving God and is held back from believing in Him when life doesn't turn out how we hoped, dreamed, or planned.

"Just trust Him. It's just Jesus," the man at our table to the left of us said.

"What does someone else think?" one of the facilitators asked as they tried to redirect the group dynamic.

"It's Jesus, just Jesus," the man said again with a slight southern drawl.

"For a lot of people, it isn't that simple," said the other facilitator. "At least not yet."

I looked over at Laurie, and we both give one another a cold hard stare with the slightest of eye rolls as if saying to one other, "You put him in the choke hold, and I'll punch him in the gut the next time he tells me it's 'just Jesus'."

Eventually, very slowly, and not with the help of the 'It's just Jesus' guy, my anger began to dull just a tiny bit...only for my frustration to grow...the frustration of how does one believe? How do you surrender yourself to someone with whom you're still pissed? Laurie, the other members at the table, the facilitators, and the pastoral staff all seemed to give me the answers I needed, which was really not to give me any actual answers at all.

Because isn't this true faith?

I ended the class with some new friends, excellent education, and in many ways, more questions than when I started.

But something had begun to shift.

God – 1

Justine – 3

Is it supposed to feel like this much of a struggle?

Without faith no one can please God
because the one coming to God must
believe He exists, and He rewards those
who come seeking.
Hebrews 11:6

Chapter 5

I'm pretty good at getting people pregnant.

After a long day of seeing clients and ending on a tough session, I walked into the house while I forced myself to take deep breaths...the deep breaths that are meant to help calm you from the inside out, but that in those moments, only make the tenderness take a more searing foothold inside your heart. Our three little dogs (yes, we're little dog people) greeted me with their absolute, infectious joy as I sat on the hardwood floor to allow them the opportunity to love all over me while still making sure I continued to breathe deeply. Yes, we are those dog people, too. We let them jump and love on everyone.

Chad could see my struggle immediately, despite the joy that overcomes me as the dogs showered me with kisses, jumps, and yips of love. "Hard sessions?" he asked.

"This book has to be published," I replied, trying to hold back the tears.

Chad took a seat on our bright orange couch in his calmness and waited for me to gush forward with my feelings. Thank God for his calm presence in my life and his willingness to always listen to my overwhelming emotion. He indeed is the Prozac to my storm.

"Women are completely losing themselves and destroying their lives. It is not about the big publisher anymore, and it's never been about the money. It just needs to be in people's hands," I said through tears, attempting to hold back the body-stealing sobs. "The infertility journey leaves so many of us ravished, as shells of who we once were and questioning every part of who we have become because of it, with the full knowledge that we will never be able to go back. And, I have to do something."

Chad looked at me with all the love and understanding I needed. He nodded in agreement and said, "Let's write this book."

And so I did.

"I cheated on my husband," She said avoiding eye contact and moving her arms around her middle as if to hold herself together.

I leaned forward, "Okay, can you tell me what happened for you?"

As she went into her background, she talked about a happy marriage pushed to the max with a few years of trying (unsuccessfully) to have a baby. A diagnosis that laid the blame on her body, since it was unable to do what we all think a woman's body is meant to do...and a mistake that she knew was not like herself and would never happen again.

"What do you think it was about for you?" I asked her with love in my eyes and accountability in my voice.

"I deserve the hurt, the shame, the guilt, and the consequences," came her sullen replied.

"So you punished yourself by making a mistake that is not who you are or who you want to be?" I asked in an attempt for her to see the truth that lies behind her suffering.

No answer, only tears.

"Do you think you may have also done it to mar yourself?" I asked knowing these words would be difficult to hear but just may be her truth. "You now have given him a reason to leave you because you can't make him a father?"

Her response came in broken down tears with a deep knowing breath.

Working with infertility clients feels like a gift to my career. It is one that did not come without the cost of loss, but also one that I have worked to be open enough to receive. Each time a woman calls me seeking support, no matter where she is in her infertility journey, I feel grateful…grateful to both witness and help her through the journey of hard work. Grateful also because this gift honors my three lost babies.

Sitting in my warm office, holding enough space for love and change, I asked the difficult questions to my infertility clients: "How far are you willing to go? What is everything you must do before you can stop, walk away, and accept?"

This is what I call our enoughs and everythings.

What is enough for you to be able to walk away?

What is everything you feel you must do to let it go?

What happens when it does not turn out how you hoped or dreamed?

For many of us, the infertility journey never turns out how we hoped, dreamed, or even paid for. Working with clients by sharing parts of my dark journey shines the light forward for them to walk through their own darkness. Together, we wrestle our way through questions that many will never have to consider.

How many rounds will we do?

How much money can we spend?

How much are we willing to spend?

How much loss and waiting can we take?

Can we be okay with the past and in our present?

Can we learn to be okay whether or not we get what we want or what we hope for?

In the work of self-forgiveness, self-care, and simple (albeit hard as hell) talk therapy, many of my clients find their way back to who they are and who they want to be.

"What do you think about scheduling?" I always asked at the end of each session, and it usually isn't very long before I hear the magic words: "I'm feeling pretty good. How about a few weeks out?"

To be honest, working with my infertility clients typically does not last long, as one of two things usually happens:

1. They do the work and begin to feel better.
2. They get pregnant.

As it turns out, I am pretty good at getting people pregnant. Chad also said I need to word this differently.

God – 2

Justine – 4

Yep, we both got a point here.

But now that we have died to those chains that imprisoned us, we have been released from the law to serve in a new Spirit-empowered life, not the old written code.
Romans 7:6

Chapter 6

I can trust the story you have written for me, and it is my job to find my place in it.

Explorations had been over for a few weeks, and my heart and brain were still reeling and fighting against one another. That next Sunday's service was titled, "Faith." Another Sunday, another service where tears streamed down my face through each of the songs and Chad hedged hit bets of whether or not a hand on my back would help or make the tears turn to sobs.

"May our hearts be not of stone, and give us souls that never close."

I bent down to grab my journal so fast that I'm sure I scared the people standing around me. My pen moved across the page so quickly people probably thought I was crazy. Tears stung my eyes as I placed my journal back down on the floor after writing down the moving lyrics. Chad glanced down at me and put his hand on the small of my back. He knew exactly what just happened.

The speed of my body dropping fast to the ground to grab the journal and the rate of the sloppy handwriting can only mean one thing! I had a blog idea, and I had to write it down.

I could feel the knot forming in my throat as Pastor Greg spoke about, how believing and having faith, doesn't mean it is all good from here on out. It merely means you trust He has the end of your story.

What the hell is this? Could I actually believe? Am I His?

Something had shifted. I don't know what and once again, I am left with more questions than answers.

I barely get out of the car when I blurted out, "I am so frustrated!"

"What is it?" he asked with his stoic patience.

"I think I trust that He has the end of my story, but I'm still pissed," I said as my voice started to shake and the volume increased drastically all at once. "I mean, is it really possible to accept Jesus *and* truly trust God *and* have doubt or be angry?"

"Maybe it is, but I honestly don't know," Chad replied, trying his very best to help me get there, while also allowing me to take the journey on my own.

I didn't sleep well that night, giving me less than ample energy to confront the busiest day of my workweek with clients. I was forced to set aside my faith crisis to provide the care that my clients deserved, but my prayers remained the same: *Please God, show this to me in a way I can understand. Please.*

In a fit of frustration, I made myself re-watch the service that next morning. Toward the end of it, Pastor Greg spoke the words I had already heard him said once, "Some of you will never fully know how much you can trust God until you commit and then you begin to see what it is to be sustained by Him. Then, you get to keep working on those doubts and questions inside your faith."

I skip back to listen to his words again, "Some of you will never fully know how much you can trust God until you commit and then you begin to see what it is to be sustained by Him. Then, you get to keep working on those doubts and questions inside your faith."

I pushed pause on my laptop computer and looked out of the floor-to-ceiling windows to the yard that I loved and yet loathed in how much work it had taken to restore and also had graced me with the best memories these last few years.

Turning my life over, knowing I am at the end of me and You have it all, does not mean in the least bit that I never doubt and question or even be angry with You.

God, I don't always have to like the life you have given to me, or have planned for me, but I can still trust it.

I know I can trust the story You have written for me, and that it is my job to find my place in it.

My body collapsed forward, my face in my hands, as I heaved with body shaking sobs. This time, however, they were healing cries of freedom.

Finally.

After a few minutes, I wiped away the tears and opened my Bible. The book that found me through *Explorations*, the book in which I have sought answers, the book that has also been the bane of my existence.

Inside the front cover, I took a deep breath and wrote the following words: "May 6th, 2014, Jesus has my everything."

Almost instinctively, I reopened my computer and went to my church's website where I clicked the "Baptism" application.

I, Justine Brooks Froelker, an unlucky, childless mother who is pretty pissed at God on some (sometimes most) days was going to declare to the world that I am with Him and He is with me.

God – 4

Justine – 4

Tied, a sliver of clarity counts for 2 for Him.

I want you to know that the Eternal your God is the only true God. He's the faithful God who keeps His covenants and shows loyal love for a thousand generations to those who in return love Him and keep His commands.
Deuteronomy 7:9

Chapter 7

"Oh we're even, I assure you! I now have also seen things that I can never unsee!"

I felt the icy trickle of sweat run down my back as I stood in front of my oldest friend, Kelly. I clutched her hands with a grip so hard I was just hoping to steady us both with it. The sterile hospital room felt stuffy, but I figured it was just my nervousness that made it feel claustrophobic. I was supposed to be feeling that icy sweat trickle down my back as a warning shot before the quick turn of my queasy stomach in the delivery of my children.

I was supposed to be the one preparing to deliver three beautiful babies. I was supposed to see them take their first breaths. Instead, here I was, waiting for the birth of my oldest friend's first daughter, waiting to see her baby girl take her first breath.

The stark florescent lighting, combined with the stuffy heat of the room, only made my heart beat faster. The nurses kept the conversation light as we had already been there for over 10 hours waiting for Kelly's labor to progress. As I knelt down, I realized that I was the one getting lightheaded. I squeezed her hand as I moved through several deep breaths. My stomach churned as the heat washed over my body and my eyes got fuzzier.

Shit. Pull it together! Deep breath. Don't fail her now. She's the one getting a needle in her spine! I shouted in my head.

With a quick flip of her hand and pressing eye contact, Kelly beckoned her husband Mike over to take my place, knowing I was at the edge of passing out cold.

Because she is that friend–the friend that often knows us better than we know ourselves.

Several months before that day, I stood in my great room in Saint Louis. During our morning phone call, while Kelly drove to work back home, up in Iowa, I told her, "I just pulled out an old picture of us from 1985 for throwback Thursday."

"Ooh, which one is it?" she asked.

"It looks like we were in a mechanical hot air balloon, like at Chuck E. Cheese or something. You look adorable, and I, on the other hand, look like a boy."

"Oh yeah, I have a blue sweater on, don't I?"

Seriously, she remembers it all, even the parts I may want to forget.

Kelly is, and always has been, my childhood friend who has seen me through the darkest of times, literally helping me bathe and go to the bathroom while in a body cast from having two back surgeries in high school. Never one to shy away from reminding me of how funny it was for us, as two high school girls, doing what we had to do. She held my unbendable body across the toilet waiting for me to poop as I was trapped in a body cast. The wait was never short with all those pain medications. She would giggle saying, "Any more rabbit turds for now?"

She is my faithful friend as she let me go when I chose to leave for college out of state, away from everyone else. She was my adventurous friend who moved to the big city of Saint Louis with me after college. She is my humble and forgiving friend as we survived a terrible falling out when we allowed boys to get in the way of our friendship like so many girls do. She is my family. We have survived tragedy together when Kelly lost her father and also years later when my father nearly died after falling off a ladder. She is my fellow warrior in fighting for her family and understanding the difficulties of infertility.

Kelly and Mike were struggling to conceive, just as our journey of infertility ended without the desired outcome of babies.

Please God, not them, too.

Hearing Kelly describe to me the transmutation of a chromosome that Mike has was much like when Chad explains his budget reports and all his meetings at work to me after a long day.

"Bottom line it for me Kel," I had said through anticipation.

Blankly, flat, as if to protect herself from the worst news possible, she responded, "It will be impossible to have our own children without In Vitro Fertilization (IVF)."

Shit.

The long road of the infertility journey is treacherous and one that should never be traveled alone. Chad and I were open with our friends and family for the most part through our journey with a gestational surrogate, and yet, knowing what I know now as an advocate and therapist working for, and in, the broken silence, I now realize we were not open enough. We needed more support as tens of thousands of dollars, timelines, waiting games, and more emotional and financial stress than you can ever imagine threatened to destroy our dreams and our relationship.

In her struggle, I made sure Kelly knew I was right alongside her. I texted Chad, "Sitting in the driveway in the car talking to Kelly, be inside in a while." while talking to Kelly, so he would know why I hadn't come inside yet. Kelly and I would regularly talk on my commute home from seeing patients in my mental health private practice. Our conversations were never short, as there were so many agonizing decisions in the infertility journey to discuss and consider.

"Where are things now? What are they saying?" I'd always asked Kelly for an update on the most recent tests.

Throughout Kelly and Mike's journey to conceive, I was able to provide that soft landing spot, especially for those difficult questions.

How many rounds do we do?

How do we know we have done enough?

What if we have leftover embryos?

How much testing should be done on the embryos?

What if the embryos are not healthy?

How do you really feel about adoption?

What about embryo adoption?

And I would listen to her each day, only responding with the occasional, "I know, it sucks!" because there is nothing more one can really said.

Months, which can seem like years later, especially in the infertility journey, it doesn't matter, here we are, having spent the last ten to twelve hours keeping Kelly entertained while her labor progressed.

"Don't you wish we had these phones during my back surgeries?" I asked.

We looked up funny YouTube videos. I danced. I sang, and Mike... well, he's just Mike. He is one of the most loving and kindest guys with a great sense of humor and intelligence, both of which intimidate me at times, Mike is also easily humbled by how human he is in his 'much bigger than me' body and his difficulty in maintaining control over it. Without a doubt, Mike could always injure himself somehow, quite possibly even in a padded room.

"What would we do without Google or YouTube?" Mike agreed.

About 12 hours in, we were all exhausted. Kelly's body was so ravaged by her labor that her doctors had allowed to go on for way too long and she was quickly losing what strength she had left. Mike and I were exhausted from high anxiety, sleep deprivation, and endless effort to help keep Kelly's anxiety down during those last hours of labor. We spent her active labor in particular jobs: Mike, at Kelly's head, fanning her and talking into her ear and me, along her side holding her leg up during pushes.

Between her painful pushes, I would make jokes to get her to laugh. "I know your vagina has got to hurt, especially by the look of it, but my arm is getting pretty tired too."

Because this is what we do. This is what we have always done – we laugh, and we love one another through it.

"You owe me. I took you shit for a whole summer!" she growled out of clenched teeth in labor pain, but still with the sparkle in her eye in which I have come to see home.

"Oh, we're even, I assure you! I now have also seen things that I can never unsee!" I joked back in all seriousness of just how insane the woman's body is during pregnancy and labor.

"Is it that bad?"

"Oh, it's bad Kel. It's bad. Your swollen vagina is even with my body cast shit."

On that day in May, under unflattering fluorescent lights and after too many hours of hard and scary delivery, Kelly and Mike's first daughter, Abigail, took her first breath of this earth's fresh air. In the split second of pure joy I felt at the sight of her beautiful face, dark hair, and healthy wail, I felt the twinge of my own longing...the longing for my three babies. She did it, and I helped. Their daughter was born with her beautiful, serene face and my chosen family grew.

But then tension grew, too, as the blood continued to pool.

Something was wrong. I let Mike stay with his brand new daughter while I went back to Kelly's bedside after taking a few photos of their new baby girl.

"Kelly," the doctor said. "Kelly!" she said more sternly this time. As I looked at the doctor's clearly concerned, and calm face, and Kelly's blank and white-as-a-sheet face, it was clear that Kelly was not okay.

"Kelly, I need you to push. The placenta is stuck, and I need you to push it out because if you can't, you will not like what I have to do next."

I grabbed Kelly's leg again, providing support despite the seething pain of how sore and tired my arm felt, and I begged Kelly to push.

"Come on, Kel. You can do it."

Somewhere from deep inside both of us, we would need to muster up all the strength and courage we had to get through this last stage of labor.

Her eyes rolled into the back of her head several times, and her words made no sense at all. The only intelligible words being the gratitude she had at becoming a mother after all this time and struggle, "What about skin-to-skin time?"

"Kelly," the doctor said trying to get her to focus again. "The placenta is stuck. If we don't get it out soon, we will have to take you to emergency surgery. I need you to push."

A few pushes from the exhausted mother only resulted in more blood pooling beneath her.

"Kelly, this is going to hurt. I have to reach up to try to get it out."

These were some of the worst moments of my life. My oldest friend was writhing in pain after a delivery that lasted much too long, who was exhausted and full of joy as a new mother…all with the doctor's entire forearm up inside of her trying to save her life.

Nothing, no progress.

Emergency surgery was the only option.

Joy and fear settled over me in that hospital room, as they rolled Kelly away from her brand new baby girl and her husband who she had made a father for the first time.

Please God, do not take this mother. Please God, be with the doctors and with us. Please keep Kelly safe and well.

We waited. Mike loved on his daughter. I prayed…and we waited more.

I love them and this little girl more than I ever thought possible. I could not imagine a world without either of them in it. I prayed again.

Please God, do not take this mother. Please God, be with the doctors and with us, please keep Kelly safe and well.

After surgery, Kelly was rolled back into the room and was finally able to truly see her daughter for the first time. It is a moment I will be forever grateful to be a part of.

I looked at Abigail with her dark hair and scrunched up face, my undeniable longing wholly overwhelmed by so much love. There she was, one of my new chosen children.

God – 5

Justine – 4

What a gift, a gift I'd never have unless all the shit before it came first.

When anxiety overtakes me and wor-
ries are many,
Your comfort lightens my soul.
Psalm 94:19

Chapter 8

With me, you will always be seen, you will always be known,
and you will always be loved.

Dear Abigail,

Your Mom and I have been through 30 years of friendship. We have been through things that, really, no two
friends should ever have to see within a friendship. Your
Mom helped me through some of the hardest times of
my life. I am sure we will one day share with you the
stories of how she used to care for me as my nurse
while I suffered through two back surgeries and lived
in a body cast. She loves telling the stories of how she
helped me go to the bathroom, and I will admit, they
are pretty hysterical.

On the day you blessed us all by coming into this
world, I helped your Mom through your challenging
and scary delivery. Since doing so, I now have my own
stories about your mother that involves things I just can
never unsee.

Although it was one of the more terrifying days of my
life, it was also one of the most magical days, as I know
it was for your Mom and Dad.

Abbie, your Mom and Dad fought so hard to bring you here. Through three years, they fought through frustrations, waiting games, anxieties, medical procedures, terrible side effects, misunderstandings from loved ones, and even their own debilitating fears...all to find you.

Your Mom and Dad continued this amazing fight through a difficult pregnancy and on the day of your Mom's labor and delivery, their fight only continued.

Scared of my limitations, fears, and aversions to anything medical or blood related, I pushed through it all to allow my anxiousness to become excitement and I fought alongside your Mom and Dad. I fought for them, and I fought for you.

I was so proud and honored to be there supporting, helping, and distracting them throughout your Mom's labor, but mostly, I was so proud and honored to simply witness them in their fight. I was blessed to witness your Mom's diligence in containing her anxiety and fears for your safety, your Dad's advocacy for you and your Mom's care and protection, and their ownership in how you came to be whenever any doctor or nurse asked about you.

Simply, profoundly, and wholeheartedly, I am so proud of them, and I am proud of you.

We all worked together as a team to bring you into this world, your Mom doing the most laborious work of all. At 4:40 pm, you finally graced us with the gift they'd been fighting and hoping for, for three long years. Your peaceful and perfect face, your dark brown hair, and your healthy cry brought tears of pure joy and gratitude to us all.

Throughout your Mom's labor of almost two full days, your Mom and Dad lied to me about your name, even though I asked them a million times (you will get to know I am undeniably persistent). Finally, the morning after your birth, when your Mom was feeling better, they gave me the best surprise of my life: your name. I was shocked and completely honored to learn your name was Abigail Justine.

It is with a heart full of love and honor that these are my promises to you, Abigail Justine, my namesake:

I promise to always do my very best to be that person your parents believed in and loved enough to name you after.

I promise to always be here for your Mom and Dad, for whatever they may need.

I promise to always be here for you, no matter what you may ever need.

I promise to always be your soft landing spot but to also always guide and push you when necessary.

I promise to love all of you, to always accept you, and to honor you; with me, you will always be seen, you will always be known, and you will always be loved.

Because being there with your parents throughout their journey to conceive you and being present for your entrance into this world is my ultimate enough moment.

Because you, Abigail Justine, are my ultimate ever upward.

With much love,
Your Aunt Justine

God – 6
Justine – 4

She's here, and I don't have to change the poopy diapers or be super sleep deprived!

Enlarge your house. You are going to need a bigger place;
don't underestimate the amount of room that you'll need. So build, build, build.
Isaiah 54:2

Chapter 9

What the fuck does that even mean?

She sat back in the chair with the unmistakable look of utter exhaustion written all over her face. I'd seen her on and off for years, as I do many of my clients. She is one, to whom life usually proved too hard and by all accounts, pretty unfucking fair. She is also the one who knew having a therapist like me for back up was a gift.

She took a deep breath, not out of mindfulness, out of sheer frustration. I could feel her shift in mood seep into the air and strike me in the face. I was careful not to allow it to enter my force field because we would then both be stuck.

"What would it be like for you to sit with this uncertainty?" I asked her, making sure not to sound too know-it-all. "Can you create enough room to feel them both, to feel it all, the anger with the joy, the sadness with acceptance, fear with bravery, the dark with the light?"

She rolled her eyes, "What the fuck does that even mean?" she spat out through semi-clenched teeth.

"What if this feeling of 'lost-ness' is actually where your magic, your clarity, hell, even your healing, lies?"

Her eyes filled with tears as the deep breath turned into one of slight relief as she allowed the words to settle into her soul.

This is the work I offer my clients. This is the work I wrestle with every damn day myself.

It's really annoying and hard, and where our truth can and will be found.

God – 6

Justine – 5

Because the Complicated Gray is fucking brutal.

but it is something you should rejoice in. In it you share the Anointed's sufferings, and you will be that much more joyful when His glory is revealed.

1 Peter 4:13

Chapter 10

"Doctor, I can't work without my smell."

Sitting in the stark white exam room with my parents was unnerving for a few reasons. First, it brought back memories of the countless hours we spent when I was 12, looking for a diagnosis for my pain before my broken spine was discovered. Second, in just a few dreaded moments, my Dad's life was going to change drastically at the young age of 57. He had fallen off a 6-foot ladder and hit every rung on the way down, landing with his forehead on the core drill bit.

I sat on the bench along the wall looking at my exhausted and worried Mom, who was looking at my Dad, who was still in immense pain from the fall. I was overcome with both gratitude that I could be here, and worry about what prognosis awaited us. The exam chair did not recline enough for my Dad to get comfortable, as he was experiencing debilitating vertigo and extreme head pain from his multiple skull fractures.

"Do you need to lie down?" I asked him.

"Can we turn off the lights at least?" he whispered.

I got up and dimmed the lights.

Just as I was about to sit back down, the doctor walked in with his intern. Both of them wearing 'untouchable' white coats that made the room feel even less safe for all of us. "Let's go through the CT," he said as he pulled up the images on the computer screen. "Here are the nasal cavity fractures," he said as he pointed to several transparent black spaces between the white bones of my Dad's forehead.

"These are the ones we have to watch closely, right?" I asked, with an undertone of fear in my voice.

"They haven't moved, which is good. But yes, if you have any sign of fluid draining out of your nose, go to the ER immediately," he said very matter of factly. "And, no sneezing through your nose or blowing your nose for six more weeks."

He clicked the mouse on the computer as more scan images appeared on the screen.

"There are about six to eight fractures around each eye. These will heal with rest," he continued.

My Dad shifted in his chair as my Mom asked, "Are you okay?"

"Just getting queasy," he replied as he took a deep breath.

"It is hard to see the scans, I know, but we need you to understand the extent of your injuries," the doctor said in his routine medical tone.

He went on to show Dad's two other skull fractures and brain bleeds.

"Overall, you are very lucky. Rest is what you can do for now. Low stimulation and lots of sleep. The brain needs to repair itself."

"What about work? We will need your help with disability," my Mom said, interrupting the doctor. Both of my parent's incomes depended on my Dad's HVAC business. I could tell the bills and the unforeseeable amount of time off work was beginning to scare her. I have no doubt it would also scare my Dad more if he weren't in so much pain.

"Yes, of course, we will help with all that paperwork."

"What about long-term?" my Dad piped up.

"I can't tell you a timeline right now."

"I can't smell still," my Dad informed the doctor.

"Okay, we will test that. Most likely, it is permanent. A round of steroids is the only course of treatment we can try. I will give you that script today," the doctor reassured him. "You will need to be careful always to have working smoke alarms and clearly mark your food with dates."

"Doctor, I can't work without my smell."

Finally, you could tell with that statement the doctor understood the gravity of no smell for my Dad. Suddenly, he realized that his cautionary tale of the life changes my Dad would have to make after losing his sense of smell meant more towards what he did for a living, and not just getting sick from eating spoiled food.

"I have to be able to smell gas and Freon," my Dad continued as if he had to fight for the doctor's support.

"Oh no, you are right. Let's see if the steroids help at all, but I want to let you know the chances are slim."

And with that, my Dad heard that at age 57, the only career he had ever known was over.

And, all our lives were forever changed by a freak accident fall off a ladder.

God – 6

Justine – 6

Tied again. Why do bad things happen to good people?

We are confident that God is able to orchestrate everything to work toward something good and beautiful when we love Him and accept His invitation to live according to His plan.
Romans 8:28

Chapter 11

"I know it's annoying, but this shit works."

My parents, who have lived their entire lives in the small Iowa town in which I grew up, had always planned to retire to Saint Louis with Chad and me in about five years time. The accident pushed this up for sure. Chad and I were in Saint Louis, without kids, where we would have the resources to take care of Mom and Dad for however long needed. The best part of this living arrangement was that they would be near an international airport to jet off to see their grandkids as my brother-in-law is in the Air Force and his career often takes the family to many far away and surprising places.

What was not in this plan was to have them here in Saint Louis so soon, or to have them living with us in the same home. It was decided mom and dad would move in with me and Chad. It didn't take long for word to travel around our small town about mom and dad picking up and leaving due to all of the accident recovery demands.

"Hey, I got a message from Ben from high school," I told my Mom.

"What?" she asked confused.

"Apparently, the word is out. He has been looking for a home in Durant for a while now and heard you guys are going to be selling."

"Well, that was fast."

Their house sold about two weeks later.

In total, Mom and Dad lived with us for eleven months almost to the day.

Parents as roommates.

In the bedroom right across the hall from us.

At only 35 years old.

It was fun and frustrating, a blessing and a curse, and something I would not trade for the world. We both needed each other immensely in that stage of our lives.

Recovery from a traumatic brain injury is active for the first two years after the injury. Dad's recovery required a lot of appointments the first year not including therapy and self-care rehabilitation from yours truly. My parents needed us as much as we needed them. My first book, *Ever Upward*, had just been published and my private practice was busier than ever. On top of that, Chad had gotten an incredible (but very unexpected) promotion at his job. We could really use the live-in help around the house, especially with the dogs.

And so began our arrangement. Mom and Dad helped with the housework, yard work, pool, and dogs...and we provided them with a home.

Having Mom and Dad move in with us was good and hard, the time was filled with annoyances, frustrations, lots of fun and everything in between. What was most prevalent during those

11 months was laughter. Well, besides my constant learning about myself. This was true mostly because having your parents as roommates means you are living with two other people who are the epitome of the personality characteristics of yourself that drive you the craziest.

My Mom is a caretaker. Always. She really enjoys taking care of others and tends to struggle with sometimes setting boundaries around it.

My Dad is passionate. Very passionate! His passion can either be unbridled joy or complete agitated anger depending on his level of self-care and the topic. And, well, I got both of these characteristics to the millionth degree.

They are my greatest strengths and when I am not careful and not doing my shit (a.k.a. self-care), they are my weaknesses.

"I am sorry I yelled," I texted to both of my parent's phones. "It's okay," they both replied.

It had been a rough morning. Nothing in particular, just more so in the energy of the day and in the house. Mom and Dad were under massive amounts of stress with doctors appointments, and therefore the bills and daily frustrations of Obamacare…more so, the administration of it versus the care of it. Such a crux. I am thankful they have insurance, and yet, it seems to have been the biggest pain in the ass ever.

But Dad needed to keep up with his therapies and continue to recover from the TBI (Traumatic Brain Injury), so we kept fighting with a medical and insurance system that seemed to be against us.

Their frustration, sharing a house, and my stress of the book and my clients culminated that morning into short, brash phrases before I semi-stormed out the door to the office.

After seeing several clients, I came home to find them in the basement watching a show with all three dogs lounging on their laps.

"I am sorry about this morning," I started. "I need you guys to do your work too."

They both looked at one another and smirked, "What do you mean?"

"I mean you are stressed too, but you aren't managing your stress. TV doesn't count for healthy coping."

"I'm relaxed," Dad retorted.

"The energy is tense and stressed, and it is affecting my recovery," I said. "I have to be better myself, and I am asking for you both to do your stuff, too."

"Color and exercise and everything else on the list?" Dad replied in a joking manner even though I knew he knew it was what was needed, both for his continued TBI recovery and also for all of our sanities.

"I know it is annoying, but this shit works. You know it does."

"We'll try."

"How about you start now and put on Alpha-Stim?" I said as I pulled out the medical device that helps to treat anxiety, depression, and stress.

"Oh geez, fine," he said.

And, right then and there, the daughter had become the parent, the therapized therapist who was therapizing them all while needing to remember to make an appointment with her therapist STAT.

God – 6

Justine -7

Did Jesus seek counsel? I mean surely one of His disciples was a Licensed Therapist or Social Worker.

Where do you think your fighting and endless conflict come from? Don't you think that they originate in the constant pursuit of gratification that rages inside each of you like an uncontrolled militia? 2 You crave something that you do not possess, so you murder to get it. You desire the things you cannot earn, so you sue others and fight for what you want. You do not have because you have chosen not to asked.

James 4:1-2

Chapter 12

Welcome home, child.

We both walked into the giant church dressed in full-on black, as instructed. Our church's baptism...our church...so weird...is a full dunk-in-a-pond-behind-the-church baptism. Chad grabbed my hand because he knew I was nervous, mostly about what to expect. There were around 400 of us getting baptized. Together, we took seats all around the auditorium as the pastors prayed over us and we were asked to spend some time in prayer.

Chad and I had not prayed together much, except at meals. Praying out loud honestly still intimidates me quite a bit.

"It is not my spiritual gift," I often said to people who asked if I'd like to close in prayer.

The family sitting behind us was praying pretty loudly, and most of them were crying. Part of my brain began to compare and started to become frustrated.

Shhh, I can't hear my thoughts with God over your talking to God!

Oh, what she said was perfect!

Crap, am I not feeling the way I am supposed to be feeling?

Am I doing this right?

I took a breath and admitted to Chad, "I feel intimidated."

"You want to pray out loud?" he asked.

"No, but that's okay right?"

"Of course it is," he said as we took one another's hands, bowed our heads and closed our eyes.

After we finished our prayers, we lined up in five lines to get ready to walk down to the pond. Like a sea of black that carries the hope of a life awash in new by His grace and mercy.

A renewed hope.

A hope through Him.

We stood in line chatting with everyone around us, hearing the occasional cheer from the crowd as someone came up out of the water with a smile of freedom on his or her face. The evening was a party of sorts. Three campuses in one location, baptizing 400 people while a thousand people sit on their lawn chairs watching. It was a sight so powerful. I just know Heaven comes to a standstill to watch from above. You can feel it and scripture said it.

When it was our turn, I walked into the water with Chad and watched him get dunked first. He was baptized as a baby, as was I. But this time it was a choice, our choice. A decision to consciously said we are at the end of ourselves, we cannot do life any longer without leaning on Him and sharing it with the world. After being completely submerged in the water, Chad came out and stepped to the side as I walked down holding our pastor's wife's hand. The smile on her face was genuine and selective for each person she encountered that day. Her beauty quickly took you over, until all you saw was the love in her eyes. We waded into the water where she handed me off to Pastor Greg, her husband.

My heart was pounding. My cheeks hurt from smiling, and tears were in my eyes as he said something like, "Take a breath and look around at all of these people supporting you in their faith and in yours. Soak it all in."

He placed his hands on my shoulders and upper back for support. "It is my honor to baptize you in the name of the Father, the Son, and the Holy Spirit."

With those words, they immersed me in the water.

In just a few seconds, washed in the waters, much of my fears and doubts flowed out of me.

I am His. And, He is mine.

Welcome home, child.

They brought me out of the water, and as a smile of freedom swept over my face like never before, I looked up and took a breath.

Thank you.

Chad took my hand as we walked out of the pond and back up to the church to change into dry clothes. They asked us to keep our hair wet, so people knew you came out of the waters a new person through Him all evening. My parents were there and were excited, despite not knowing exactly what this new faith thing was all about for me.

We ate tacos and the most delicious cupcakes from the food trucks as we placed our seats in the parking lot to sing along to our fantastic worship band.

Just like that, I declared my faith to the world.

He is mine, and I am His.

I had declared that even on the days I was not happy, or I was in doubt, or I questioned the story He has written for me, I would also take His gift of free will to find my place in it.

God – 10
Justine – 7 or is it 0?

Big points! In Him, through Him, and because of Him.

This is how it is in heaven. They're happier over one sinner who changes his way of life than they are over 99 good and just people who don't need to change their ways of life.
Luke 15:7

Chapter 13

"But they are not your paying clients. They are your parents."

I recounted the latest happenings of living with my parents to my therapist, Shellie. When I finished with my complaints, I sat back on her modern white leather couch ready to receive my empathy and hear, "You're so right, Justine."

Her eyes got soft before she said, "It sounds tough to adjust, for sure."

Empathy, check.

"Are you micromanaging?"

Called out on my shit, check!

"Sure am! I mean, if they would just do what I tell them to do, they would be happy and healthy!"

"But they are not your paying clients. They are your parents."

Shit.

God – 11

Justine – 8 or 1 (depends on how you count it)

Is this getting too complicated?

People do their best making plans for their
lives, but the Eternal
guides each step.
Proverbs 16:9

Chapter 14

"I swear I took my clean underwear into the bathroom for my shower."

"What was Chad doing home this morning?" my Dad asked with a look of confusion laced with the ease of trying to appear nonchalant.

"He had his doctor's appointment this morning before work, remember? Why?" I replied, worried if it was going to be one of those days with his TBI.

"He messed with my morning routine."

"See! Not that awesome is it? But, wait, what do you mean exactly?"

Dad smirked and took a deep breath before going on, "Every morning I go and weigh myself in your guys' bathroom...in my underwear."

I smiled and nodded because I knew this. Since living with us, mom and dad's health was changing drastically by being consistent on his Plexus supplements, walking the dogs, and eating better. This, also, couldn't possibly be going where I thought it was.

My Dad continued, "I thought it was weird that the door was closed and there was Chad in the shower!"

Laughing hysterically, I managed to get out, "So, you saw my husband naked?!"

"Yep, sure did. I told you it messed with my morning routine!"

The whole day Chad had never mentioned it, even when we got home that evening. "So how about that whole, my-Dad-seeing-you-naked-this-morning-thing?" I said, probing for something from my stoic husband.

"I was squeegeeing the shower doors and thought you were coming in, and there was your Dad in his towel and his tightie-whities. He looked at me with a shocked face and walked right back out."

"Um, awkward, and sorry!" I replied without any attempt to maintain my composure. "He feels pretty embarrassed I think."

And, in his classic unflappable Chad that he is, he replied, "Do you know how many guys I have seen naked or have seen me naked as an athlete growing up? Not that big of a deal!"

This was Chad, often in his silent reverie and mellow demeanor, the entire year that Mom and Dad lived with us. It was not uncommon for people to asked us how things were going and Chad would replied, "I think it is harder for Justine a lot of the time than me."

He is a rock, my firm foundation for so many parts of my life to my feel-everything-to-the-extreme earthquake a lot-ness.

And unfortunately, it was not the only instance involving my Dad in his underwear…

I was making our morning smoothies when I heard my Dad yell down the hall, "Justine?" in a somewhat panicked voice.

"Yea!" I yelled back in our classic Brooks family volume of much too loud for such a small space. And, of course, just as it is anyone's instinct, I turned to look and moved toward where he was yelling my name. As I turned, I simply heard a scampering of feet down the hall and a slam of Mom and Dad's bedroom door.

That's weird, I thought to myself and continued with making our breakfasts.

Moments later, my Dad came down the hall and into the kitchen and said, "I think I may be having a TBI moment."

"What's up?" I asked with concern.

"I swear I took my clean underwear into the bathroom for my shower," he said with a look of utter confusion on his face.

As it became clear to me, I realized that my Dad was most likely scampering down the hallway either naked or in his dirty underwear after yelling my name. Holding back a bark of laughter, I said, "Next time you need to race back to your bedroom mostly naked, don't yell my name so I won't come looking!"

It wasn't until a while later that we found that pair of underwear in the middle of the great room floor. Still so confused, my Dad started to have one of those moments of *oh shit this TBI crap is serious*, so I had to remind him, "Remember, you live in a house with three dogs now, two of which are endlessly curious. If you don't close a door, they will come in and steal whatever is on the floor, including your underwear."

With the relief that he was not losing his mind in a TBI moment, he smiled lovingly as he said, "Damn it Gertie and Gracie!" before he scooped them up onto his lap.

They are not grandkids, but I have no doubt my parents love our three, the three furry ones here on earth and our three in heaven, with all their hearts.

Although they will never get to see us parent our children here on earth, having Mom and Dad stay with us for 11 months provided many opportunities for me to parent them.

Whether or not any of us liked it.

The child was parenting her parents. That is some mucky and messed up Complicated Gray, as most of these moments were extremely difficult. Given the difficulties, we were all thankful for the moments that were humorous and light, especially the ones around the dinner table.

After our infertility journey, I changed my entire life, including my diet. The synthetic hormones of the journey had wreaked havoc on my body; 35 pounds heavier and all my meds had stopped working. I began following the Blood Type Diet and still do, along with my Plexus supplementation now. This healthy eating was not how I grew up, and we all knew it might be the toughest adjustment when Mom and Dad moved in with us.

"Don't expect to eat dinner with each other every night."

This was almost always the first line of advice we would get when people learned that my parents were moving in with us.

I typically see clients two nights a week in my private practice. Which means I scramble a simple dinner like deli turkey and veggies (and the occasional popcorn) when I get home, all while surrounded by the wafts of delicious Iowa food that Mom had cooked for them since I worked later.

"Well, we have to feed your husband yummy food when we can," Mom would said referring to the fried white potatoes, Iowa pork chops and corn she made for dinner that night.

"Corn is not a vegetable!"

"And, neither is iceberg lettuce, so that doesn't count!"

These were typical dinnertime conversations/arguments at the table.

"You can always tell where you sit," were Chad's words throughout our marriage, referring to what a messy eater I am. After Mom and Dad moved in, these words quickly changed into, "Justine and Linda's seats are always the messiest; seriously how does this happen?"

One particular evening, as we were all preparing dinner, I said, "Let's eat out on the patio tonight, it's gorgeous out."

The dogs played and ran around the pool while the four of us sat around the patio table with our chicken, rice and for that night's veggie, a bag of frozen cauliflower and broccoli. Mom had already taken the world's smallest portion of the vegetables, to which she saw my look and said, "At least I am trying it."

One bite in and we all knew she was not going to be getting her vegetable portion for the day in her dinner. All of a sudden, Chad got a glimmer in his eye and said, "If you eat this small scoop, we'll go get ice cream."

She laughed, along with the rest of us, because we all knew it was the best way to get her to eat her veggies...and eat them she did. Sure, she smashed them between two saltine crackers, but she still technically ate them.

After dinner that night, we bought ice cream, well, technically, frozen yogurt.

For eleven months, I parented and was taken care of. For eleven months, my parents let me help and still took care of their daughter. It was some of the most challenging times of our relationship, and the best.

Little did I know, it wouldn't last as long as I had hoped.

God – 12

Justine – 8 or 1

This time with mom and dad, something I will never take for granted.

Teach a child how to follow the right way;
even when he is old, he will stay on course.
Proverbs 22:6

Chapter 15

Only because I asked and she invites.

"Come on, Lane!" I screamed at the top of my lungs as I held the shutter button so as not to miss the perfect shot.

He scurried down the soccer field, his legs much shorter than all the other four-year-old boys and his arms working overtime to propel him forward.

"Lane, it's open, go for the goal!" Lane's Mom, Sam, shouts even louder.

I laughed as I clicked the camera in the sports mode to ensure I got some excellent shots of the missed goal and the four-year-old collision on the field.

When the game ended, no score truly kept, Lane came over with a smile so wide it was brighter than the warm sun that day.

"Did you see my goal?" he asked his Mom and Dad.

"It was awesome Lane!" both Seth and Sam exclaimed. "Great job buddy! Now, thank Justine and Chad for coming to watch your game!"

"Thank you," he said as he crashed into me with a full body force hug.

One of many games we would see of Lane and his brothers, Noah and Evan, during their entire childhood, only because I asked and because my friend, Sam, always invited.

Just months earlier, Chad and I had been at the church musical of Lane's older brother, Noah.

"We have seats in the third row," Sam had texted me.

Chad and I walked into the huge church audience, the only couple without kids, and slid down the row to take our seats right alongside Noah, Lane, and Evan's two sets of grandparents.

We are not their aunt and uncle, officially, and yet, just as much a part of the family.

Noah beamed on stage while he sang, "We're going back, we're going back, we're going back to the cross!" He moved perfectly in sync with the music. I looked down the row to Sam, both of us smiling with pride, full of amusement, and both of us with our cameras snapping video and pictures of Noah in his element.

One woman their mother, the other a childfull mother.

God – 13

Justine – 8 or 1

Two mothers, very different mothers, who see one another.

Into the home of the childless bride,
He sends children who are, for her, a cause
of happiness beyond measure.
Praise the Eternal!
Psalm 113:9

Chapter 16

Killer sperm cells

I returned a quick text message to a client when I saw my notification light in my office light up, letting me know that my next session was here. I walked fast and loud because I didn't know how to do it any other way, down the hall and opened the heavy door to my warm, lamp-lit, water fountain-soothing waiting room. "Hey, come on back," I said with a smile.

There was something in her eye as she turned her head slowly towards me, made eye contact, and got up to come back to my office.

She's pregnant.

"What's going on? How are things?" I asked as we both sat down in our perspective spots—me, in the polka dot chair and her, in the navy floral chair looking out my tree house-like windows.

She shifted her eyes down but had the slightest smirk on her face.

She is definitely pregnant!

"What is going on? Everything okay?" I asked her again.

"I'm pregnant," she said with the entire gamut of emotion in her voice.

"What? Oh my gosh! That is so exciting! And, hard! How? What? Oh my gosh! Fill me in!" My love and excitement caused me to shout these words at her at top speed. After three years of nothing and several rounds of treatments and no baby, we had been working on her acceptance and letting go of the dream of children.

"I know, right? I was so nervous to tell you. I mean it is amazing, but it does not feel fair."

"Never. I appreciate your concern for my feelings, but this is amazing news. I am so, so, so happy for you guys," I reassured her.

"But you deserve it, too."

"Most of us do, I guess…but I'm okay, I promise. Truly, I am so excited! Now, fill me in!"

"It is crazy. I mean, with my killer sperm cells and literally nothing, even with medicated cycles, and we get pregnant without even trying? It is crazy!"

"It is amazing! How do you feel? It can still be weird and scary for a bit, especially after all this time of trying."

"I know. I am still feeling guilty. I am scared too…happy, but scared. What if something happens?"

"It could. We both know that. Unfortunately, infertility takes away our freedom and ability to be happy without a care in the world, even when pregnancy does happen. We've already experienced the worst case scenario, and so we have to embrace both the joy and the fear. You will be feeling both, for probably, the whole pregnancy until you have that baby in your arms," I explained to her.

Her eyes began to fill with tears with what I knew was the sense of overwhelm and calm that envelopes us when we give ourselves permission to feel what we have been taught are two opposing emotions.

I went on, "There is room for both fear and joy, all at the same time, I promise. Not easy to feel or even to wrap your brain around, but you can give yourself permission to feel both of them."

I saw her for a few more weeks after that, through most of her first trimester. Until one day she said what I knew was coming: "I don't think I need to come back."

"I know."

"Of course, I will call when I need to, but I think I am okay."

"You are, and I will always be here if you need anything. Please, let me know when that baby gets here."

"Thank you."

"You're welcome."

The see-you-later when a client feels strong enough to do this life in her most authentic and healthy way without me, by herself, is not unlike what a mother must feel when dropping her child off at the first day of college.

God – 14
Justine – 9 or 2

Are you still keeping up?
Thank you, God, for giving me this story to help others…
and, dammit that I don't get the baby, too.

Place your trust in the Eternal; rely on Him completely;
never depend upon your own ideas and inventions.
Give Him the credit for everything you accomplish,
and He will smooth out and straighten the road that lies ahead.
Psalm 3:5-6

Chapter 17

"You're our red shirt."

I took the lead, as I usually do when we walk anywhere, whether or not I know where I'm going. Chad usually lets me stomp forward at lightning speed, knowing full well that we are headed in the wrong direction until I turn around and said something like, "Wait, is this right?" My excuse for walking super fast and with purpose is that I have people to see and things to do and I've had to do them with super short legs my whole life.

Walk faster!

That Sunday was no different. I like a particular section of our large church auditorium, and I was going to make sure we got those seats. In my purposeful rush, I missed who was sitting directly behind us.

"Justine!" she nearly screamed, with eyes lit up that I kind of feel like a celebrity, or as Chad likes to said, "Minor celebrity here".

"Hi, honey!" I replied to my 12-year-old client and her family. "How are you?"

"So good!" they all said together.

We all settled into our seats to worship and to hear the pastor's message for the weekend.

"He will send us Jesus in skin," Pastor Greg said. To which, I grabbed my pen-with the ferocity that only a writer would recognize-to make sure I got everything down. Greg went on to tell his own scary story when he was traveling overseas, where his own Jesus in skin happened to be wearing a red shirt. He finished his message with, "Be someone's red shirt."

The lights dimmed, and the music began to close out another incredible message. When the music finished, I turn around to grab my coat and purse as I feel cold fingers on my wrist. I looked up to meet the misty eyes of my client's Mom, "You're our red shirt. Thank you for everything. You've changed our lives."

"You're welcome," I replied, as the tears filled my own eyes. I looked at my young client and smiled as she did the same.

The red shirt, Jesus in skin, in that of a childless mother.

God – 15

Justine – 9 or 2

Oh, the glimpses He gives me.

My dear brothers and sisters, stay firmly planted—be unshakable—do many good works in the name of God, and know that all your labor is not for nothing when it is for God.
1 Corinthians 15:58

Chapter 18

"She would really like to meet a real-life author,"

It was the first gorgeous day in mid-April after a long, gray Saint Louis winter and therefore not the best Saturday to hope for a big crowd in the mall to come for my first book signing.

"You excited?" Chad asked.

"I am! My first book signing, but I am weirdly calm. I think I am protecting myself from getting my hopes up too high." I replied as I pulled out my new dress from Stitch Fix.

"Ooh, I like that one," Chad said referring to the green and navy dress with a funky pattern that had just enough fun and professional in it, especially when combined with my wavy red hair. My parents, Chad and I headed to the Barnes & Noble store in Chesterfield Mall. The store manager greeted me with a big sign set up at the front of the store and a small table stacked with copies of *Ever Upward*.

"It will be an out of the park success if you sell ten books," she said with eyes that tell me she did not have high hopes, especially with the beautiful weather that day.

"Ten books. Okay, I guess we'll see," I said with an equaled measure of hope and realism.

For two hours, I sat at that little table, overwhelmed by stacks of my books. I smiled as people walked through the entrance to the store. Forty-five minutes into the signing, not one person had stopped or even made much more than the proper eye contact with me when a woman about 75 years old walked directly towards me. She picked up my book and turned it softly in her hands feeling the suede-like cover.

"All my kids had trouble having kids…they even had to do the infertility treatments," she said with an emotional disconnect I recognized all too well when it came to the pain of infertility.

"It's so hard. They may really find my book helpful then," I replied, hoping to not only connect with her but also to get that sale.

"Oh, well, it worked for them, so they don't need help anymore."

Advocate activated!

"Well, actually that is why lifelong is in the subtitle. I have found the losses, and the stresses incurred during the infertility journey can last for quite some time, if not forever," I replied mustering up all the truth in love I could find in my now activated advocate.

"Oh, well, I guess. Good luck today. I'll tell my kids about the book," she said as she walked off.

I look at Chad and my interns who were also helping and said, "Damn, thought maybe she'd buy one."

"Remember a lot of people also might go home and buy it from Amazon," said one of my interns.

Another 45 minutes passed without a stop, or a book sold, and I could feel my inner critic start to perk up in my head.

Your first and maybe only signing and you have not sold one fucking book. This is such a joke. What a waste of time and energy for everyone. You should be embarrassed.

In my next breath, I attempted to practice what I taught: gratitude.

I am grateful to be here. I am an author at her first book signing, and that is pretty amazing.

I pushed down the voice and blinked back the slightest of tears as I made eye contact with another woman approaching the table. She picked up the book and said, "I had to do infertility treatments, too. Did it work for you?" she asked with the kindest curiosity in her voice.

"It did not. We live what I call a childfull life where we are involved in our loved ones' childrens' lives. You?" I replied, already assuming I knew where this conversation was going.

"It didn't. So brutal, I wouldn't wish it on anyone. We adopted from China. What about adoption?"

Fuck. Here we go…why don't you just adopt? (but actually asked in a slightly more empathic way.)

"We've always known adoption was not right for our family. How old are your children?" I asked her, trying not to allow shame to steal my truth and instead, connecting with her as a true fellow warrior of the infertility journey.

We talked for a bit more about her amazing children, and she wished me well as she walked away from the table empty-handed.

I'm getting it, God.

I am not selling books today. Instead, I am connecting and educating.

Would still be nice to sell a damn book though, I thought as I glanced up and challenged Him.

Thirty minutes left in the book signing, two slightly tricky connections and only one book sold to a girl with whom I went to college. The inner critic was now winning. As much as I tried not to have expectations for the signing, the realization that I would sell nowhere near those ten books settled in me like a dark failure. Just as the tears threatened to come again, I took a deep breath and reminded myself to stay open to what I am supposed to receive here. As I exhaled the breath I was holding. I saw a mother with three children looking at me and whispering.

"Hi! How are you guys today?" I said with a chipper professionalism that was probably overdone as I pushed my inner critic down.

"She would really like to meet a real-life author," the Mom said as she placed her hand on top of the younger girl's head.

"Well, I guess I am a real life author now. Come on over."

"So you really wrote this book?" the girl asked with wonder and excitement that can only be gussied up as a child whose writing had not been beaten down by the critics and difficult platform building.

"How exactly do you write a book?" she nearly squealed, with a spark in her eye and a hunger to learn growling so loudly I could feel it make my heart beat a bit faster.

She went on to speak super fast, telling me she wanted to be a writer one day and that she writes every day.

"Well then, you are already a writer!" I told her. "Every day, write for at least 30 minutes a day. It's like building a muscle. Creativity has to be worked out," I told her.

As we had this 8-year-old, philosophical discussion on writing, her Mom had picked up my book to read the full title. Interrupting out of sheer excitement, "This is about IVF? They're IVF babies!!" she exclaimed placing her hands on top of each of the children's heads.

"Are you guys twins?" I asked with genuine curiosity and the knowing love of meeting another fellow warrior.

"They know exactly how much Mom and Dad had to go through to get them here," Mom replied. "Did it work for you?" she asked with the complete expectation that I would tell her about my 2.5 children.

"It didn't," I stated with simple ownership.

Her eyes filled with tears and then she leaned forward to place her hands on the table. With sad eyes, she looked up at me and said, "Oh my gosh, I am so sorry."

"Thank you, but it's okay. I am okay. That's what this book is about actually."

It's at this point that I realized how many people were watching this interaction: my two interns I was able to hire for some platform building support, Chad, my parents, and my best friend, Lindsay. The pain and love exuding from them toward us were palpable. Chad leaned down to my ear and whispered, "Give her a journal," as we were giving away our *Ever Upward* journals for free with each purchase.

I handed the girl a journal, as her Mom said that they weren't going to buy a book, "For free?!?" the little girl asked in shock.

"Only if you promise me to write in it every day for 30 minutes," I told her, "because you are a writer!"

"I promise!" she said as she leafed through the white leather bound journal graced with the breakaway monarch that also fluttered across my book cover.

"Asked if she will be your pen pal," her Mom instructed her. "I am homeschooling them next year, and she will need a pen pal for English," Mom explained to me.

"Will you?" the girl asked.

"Of course!" I said, excited for her.

No advocating. No book sale. Just pure, loving human connection. God was reminding me that this was much bigger than even I could dream. I looked at my family for the first time that day with tears of joy and no inner critic doubt or disappointment.

The day ended with only three books sold. We packed up to leave, and after going to the bathroom, my Dad said, "That little girl came by again. You should have seen her disappointment when she thought you had left already."

Out of nowhere, she ran up and wrapped her tiny little arms around me, "Thank you! Bye!"

"Thank you, and make sure to write me!" I replied.

Taking a deep breath to make room for both, a bit of disappointment and more gratitude in my soul than I have felt in a long time, this was the Complicated Gray.

God – 16

Justine – 9 or 2

I am really stubborn.

Stay focused on what's above,
not on earthly things
Colossians 3:2

Chapter 19

"A mental health therapist who can't have babies. There is not much more than that to make you pretty pissed off at God."

"I can't believe I am going to be facilitating an actual class about Christianity," I said to Chad that morning.

"I can," he replied in his usual, nonchalant demeanor.

"Really?"

"I think you are a great person to help someone else through their faith walk."

"Thanks, babe."

He kissed me goodbye and headed out the door. It was official. I would be facilitating a table at one of the best classes at our church. I was going back to the class that started it all for me: *Explorations*. I was paired with a young man I knew of in the church but had never officially met. That seemed to happen a lot at a church our size. I felt like I knew the person, but we had never met formally. Sunday before service we found ourselves sitting down to have a mini-get-to-know-you session.

"So, tell me about your faith testimony," I said to Jake. Along with an energy that is so positive, you automatically feel drawn to him. He may possibly have had the kindest expressions with which I'd ever come into contact. I also beat him to the punch because I was assuming his faith testimony was different. Scarcity and comparison tell me his story is better than mine, especially as a resident pastor at the church.

"I grew up in the church. My parents would even kick me out of their room so they could pray together. I accepted Christ when I was six years old, and I still remember the prayer I prayed. I have been attending here since I was 13 years old," he explained.

"That is incredible," I couldn't help but blurt out while also thinking to myself, *we are going to make amazing co-facilitators.*

"I got my education in all things pastor, and now I am here in my residency," Jake continued. "What about you?

"Well, I often tell people I grew up with faith and not religion," I replied truthfully.

"What? Tell me about that. I don't think I have ever heard it put that way," Jake asked with genuine confusion.

"I always knew about God, and that there was something bigger out there and that everything would be okay…but it was never through scripture or through Christ as my savior. You pair that with growing up to become a mental health therapist who can't have babies, and well, there is not much more than that to make you pretty pissed off at God."

"No kidding!" he explained, apparently amused by my response.

We were sitting at a bar height table in the lobby of our huge church. People were beginning to mill around a bit more as we got closer and closer to the service starting. This massive church with thousands of people had become my refuge the last year or so.

"After a lot of work and attending here, it all finally began to click. It wasn't until I took this class that I was finally able to open myself up enough to receive His gift. I was only able to do that by realizing that I could still doubt, question and even be angry at the story that God has given me. But, I can still trust where and how I fit into His story." I said. I swallowed hard with a bit of embarrassment because I realized tears were coming to my eyes.

"That is amazing."

"Thank you. I think it is pretty obvious why they've put us together as co-facilitators. We will provide such an incredible balance."

"I'm excited, this will be great," Jake said.

"Me too."

Little did I know how much his words, "excited, this will be great," would become part of my vocabulary with the church and with my friend, Jake.

God – 16
Justine – 9 or 3

I mean, me facilitating a church class...I am torn as to who wins the point on this one...

Do not fear, Moses. I will be with you every step of the way, and this will be the sign to you that I am the One who has sent you: after you have led them out of Egypt, you will return to this mountain and worship God.
Exodus 3:12

Chapter 20

And, at peace? Fuck that.

It had already been a year since I walked into the waters of baptism and I had volunteered to be a part of the cardboard testimony this year at church. We were asked to write a few words about our lives before accepting Christ for one side of the card and then a few words for after. I knew no one would publicly put infertility on their card, so I knew I had to volunteer. Our church is huge and very well-established, which means two things:

1. They have a system for everything. They are a well-oiled machine, and I trust them.
2. I knew I was not the only one suffering from infertility and loss.

My first submission read:
FRONT: *Shattered & invisible after loss and infertility*
BACK: *Restored & seen by Jesus in childfull light*

And then this was their first edit of it:
Front: *Heartbroken by infertility*
Back: *At peace. Trusting Him.*

And this was my first re-edit:

Front: *Shattered by infertility & loss.*

Back: *Renewed in trusting Him.*

I couldn't deal with heartbroken and at peace. Heartbroken did not seem to even touch what is left after ending the infertility journey without kids. It just does not accurately describe the lifelong loss we will suffer.

And, at peace?

Fuck that.

Moments of peace sure, more and more of them as life goes on…but at peace?

Fuck you.

Guess I still have some work to do.

I trusted my church, and I knew they were working with 25 other people to make sure there wouldn't be too much repetition of words and phrases, but, my babies made me a mother, one who was found and is more a mother because of her calling into advocacy. There was no way I was going to walk onto that stage in front of thousands of people with the word infertility on one side of my cardboard and then "at peace" on the other.

At one point, I even offered to step down and not participate.

I am a writer, so I admit, I easily get tripped up on certain words which others may only consider semantics.

I am also a woman working to thrive after life didn't turn out how she had hoped, dreamed, planned, and paid. I was not going to publicly declare that I was "at peace" when I knew instinctively that it wasn't the truth…yet.

They finally agreed to let my sign read:
FRONT: *Shattered by infertility and loss*
BACK: *Healing by trusting Him*

There were 25 of us in each service walking out on stage with our cards while our worship band played *No Longer a Slave*. The people I met that weekend, through our rising into His arms of grace and the power of sharing our stories was one of the most significant experiences in the church thus far for me.

It was nothing short of holy.

All of us in some sort of grief, the grief of life not turning out how we had hoped. The grief of a traumatic brain injury, of divorce, of the death of two daughters, of cancer, and of infertility.

The lifelong losses of grief all surrounded by the glory and holiness of Christ's gift of grace.

God – 17
Justine – Let's just call it 3

I am realizing I'm actually in this with Him.

*Then you are ready to put on your new self,
modeled after the very likeness of God:
truthful, righteous, and holy.
Ephesians 4:24*

Chapter 21

"Monarch!"

It was another sweltering Fourth of July in Saint Louis.

It was also another holiday that brought up all the same old longings.

Although this year, the third year after failed infertility treatments, it seemed as if these summer holidays could sting the most. That sharp sting that somehow feels new every time, as it brought an often-placated longing back to the surface that had been dulled by life going on and moving forward. The summers where everyone is busy with vacations and plans, but the summer holidays seem more hectic and more reserved for plans with family...families with kids. That bite of being left behind nibbled at the back of my heart.

By God, I am going to swim in my damn pool this Fourth of July even if splashing, giggling kids do not surround me.

And, I will be grateful while sad, honoring it all because if I don't make room for both, I fear I may shrivel up and die.

And so, with my chilled glass of red wine, my version of the perfect pool drink, I swam with my best friend, Lindsay, my parents, and Chad. Lindsay sat on the side of the pool with her ginormous but considered fashionable hat and toes in the water. Dad and Chad lounged on floats with beers in hand. Mom never stopped moving as she did her swim jog exercises all around the pool. All while I disrupted their relaxation with my squeals each and every time I jumped off the diving board. I couldn't help it. I loved it! So I continued with my pure joy squeals as I jumped off the diving board over and over.

I swear I could jump off that diving board for hours. I probably could do it by myself if I also didn't honestly love to be judged and receive criticism to help me always improve that next jump…the paralleled crux of so many parts of my life.

See me!

Cheer me!

Tell me how to improve!

Chad had gone inside without me noticing when all of a sudden he stuck his head out of the sliding glass door.

"Monarch!" he screamed.

Our butterfly garden was in full bloom—the calamint spilled over the wall in light green leaves and filled the air with minty scents while the butterfly bushes provided pops of color, and the joe pye weed stood gloriously over it all. Even in all this, we had yet to see a monarch flutter about. We had worked tirelessly on it in hopes of helping the monarch population and giving myself a hobby to maintain sanity.

We all scrambled out of the pool. We stumbled over one another like children coming in for dessert…and we watched her.

We watched her flutter around the garden weaving in and out of the bright blossoms and never really deciding where she wanted to grace her presence.

With a quick change of direction, she settled on a plain old milkweed leaf. We all leaned in closer to see what she was doing. Chad and I locked eyes with one another. Then, we looked back at her as we leaned closer yet.

"She's laying eggs," we whispered excitedly.

"What?" Lindsay squealed.

"Oh my gosh! She is actually laying eggs!" I was so excited, and I could hardly get the words out.

We all fell silent in awe of the miracle that was unfolding in front of us.

She came and made me a mother on a sweltering Fourth of July, another longing holiday without my babies.

I am a monarch farmer.

So freaking weird...and cool. Admit it.

My first year of farming monarch butterflies, I released 122 healthy monarchs into the wild. I posted the entire journey on Facebook and for the first time, experienced what it must be like to have adorable babies about which to post. The likes and comments came in the dozens.

I even got gifts and messages from children in my life, calling me the butterfly lady.

"I think it is going to go," I tell Chad with urgency.

I'd been researching monarch caterpillars for weeks now, and it looked like we were going to see our first one go into her chrysalis.

Using the camera on my phone, I started recording, hoping to get the beautiful process on video.

"How do you know?" Chad asked.

"Her tentacles will get limp and twisted," I replied.

We waited in anticipation, both leaning onto the granite counter in our kitchen, while we watched the white, black and yellow caterpillar prepare for its transformation.

Suddenly she straightened out completely.

"Watch for the split behind her head," I said.

"There it is," Chad said.

After about eight minutes, we saw the long white, black and yellow caterpillar reveal a bright jade green chrysalis. She writhed rather violently to make sure she was secure enough to hang for the next 10 to 14 days. She has now turned into a literal butterfly soup surrendering into the monarch butterfly she was always meant to be.

I looked at Chad, "Thank you for entertaining this super weird hobby."

"Oh, I am not entertaining anything. This is amazing," he replied. "Are you crying?"

"Yep. Yep, a little bit. That was so miraculous."

"It truly was."

The monarchs are a way I mother. Refreshing their milkweed leaves twice a day once they are big guys, cleaning up their green frass (aka poop), making sure they aren't crawling all over one another or fighting, cheering them on as they go through the tumultuous process of larvae to caterpillar to chrysalis to butterfly. Letting them go when they are ready.

Just like a Mom.

And not a Mom.

God – 18

Justine – 3

Weirdest hobby ever.

Days are coming when people will said,
"*Blessed are the infertile; blessed are the
wombs that never bore a child; blessed are
the breasts that never nursed an infant.*"
Luke 23:29

Chapter 22

"Justine!"

In the hot dead middle of the Saint Louis summer, we hold our Annual Summer Olympics party. The adults play a tournament of backyard games while the kids fill up our pool with giggles and splashes. It is a tradition I dreamed of and could already see in my head as we stood in the overgrown backyard of the hoarder house we purchased after our failed infertility journey. And this year was no different.

The grill was hot, the pool was refreshing, and the party was just about to begin, I am filled with anticipatory joy. I hear the first car door slam and know that the first bunch of kids is going to round the corner of the house at full speed with their swimming trunks already on. I also know there will be yelling by the parents, "Hold on boys, you have to put on sunscreen first!"

They all raced down to the pool area impatiently awaiting their parents to slather them with SPF 50 before they jump in the pool with the squeals I have come to love!

"Where is the slide?" Noah asked.

"It broke." I lied to him. The slide, more like "slide," from last summer was a preschool plastic toy Chad had hunkered down by the side of the pool by the jumping board in the deep end. We were lucky it lasted us a summer without significant injury, so we had decided not to put it out this summer.

"Awwwwah!" Noah whined the classic child whine that really means that's not fair!

"I am sure you will figure something else out."

The next car door slammed shut and the next three boys come running down the yard!

"Yes! The floats!" They all three said in unison and jump right in the pool.

I helped the parents, all our closest friends, set down their belongings and Chad gets everyone drinks.

This year, our 2nd annual Summer Olympics, the games seemed to be more of a bust as the adults were called to the fun of the pool as much as the kids are.

My friend Julie asked, "No water guns?"

"No water guns. I figure they are all creative enough as it is. Maybe they won't notice?"

"Right…" Julie said. We both know this is nowhere near true when you have a total of nine boys from three families all swimming in one pool.

"Where are the water guns?" Noah and Brady ran up and asked.

"We don't have any this year."

Man, I am just busting their chops this year.

"Okay."

I should have known this was too good to be true. I mean I didn't even get an awwwwah.

It was hot that day, but we all lounged around trading places in the shade or with our feet dipped in the pool when it was your turn to lifeguard all the craziness that is no less than 12 kids in the pool at once.

"Justine!" I can hear the mischief in Noah's voice, and I am almost afraid to turn around.

"What's up bud?"

Whoosh! And there it is, super cold water all over from a makeshift water bottle water gun.

See, I knew they would figure it out.

Noah ran away from my clutches as we both laugh.

As we ran towards the pool and he jumped right into the deep end cannonball style, I notice the slide the boys have made in their own accordance by draping a foam float over the jumping board. The boys are all pushing each other off it like a slide into the deep end.

"Whose idea was that, boys?"

"All of us! Isn't it awesome?" They all asked full of pride. A pride that also matches my own. My pride in the magic of this house, these people and our chosen family love.

Had IVF worked for us, we would have stayed in the county of Saint Louis with all of the other soccer moms. We would have bonded with our cul de sac friends and hung out in someone's driveway having to lug the kids just a few blocks away.

But it didn't work. So instead, we found Mason House. No cul de sac. No nursery. Just a couple of extra bedrooms, a toy room, and a pool. Room for all of the kids in our lives to come play for a while for the rest of their lives.

The child*full* life at its best.

God – 20

Justine – 3

A house full of kid craziness, yelling, laughing, crying, and a wet toilet seat. And, they all go home to sleep in their own beds!

There is nothing better than for people to eat and drink and to see the good in their hard work. These beautiful gifts, I realized, too, come from God's hand.

Ecclesiastes 2:24

Chapter 23

Why is this happening?

A florescent lit bathroom filled with her laugh and joy, you could feel it pouring from every cell of her being. I just had to pee before going on live television for my monthly interview. But I noticed her because I felt her spirit in every cell of my being.

Then I heard her story. Scleroderma, an autoimmune disease that meant essentially her soft and connective tissues would harden, most likely leading to her death much too young.

She smiled. She educated. She changed you when you met her.

And, then my phone rang later that week, she wanted to work with me, she thought I could help her.

Little did either one of us know the journey God had in store for us, together in my small sun drenched office and out in the world, especially in our faith communities.

Two people, only He could have orchestrated coming into one another's lives. To change us both so much through our own very different challenges in life, with our bodies and with our faith.

In my new wrestled for faith, I was able to introduce her to a loving God, who can handle our doubts, fears and even anger at the story He has written for us. And yet, we knew we both had the grace and clarity of Jesus and that we can trust this story even with the doubt and anger.

Through my own journey of not getting what I wanted in life, I was able to allow her to sit with, not in, the Complicated Gray of her life too.

The *this sucks. This is hard. This hurts. I want more. Hell, I deserve more. Why is this happening?* All the way until close to when she went home to be with our Father, and she said to me, *But, Justine I am really a patient now, like all of the time.*

And with tears in my eyes I said, *I know. It sucks, and you must choose to know you are more.*

Together, we struggled, survived and chose to thrive.

Often, it is the simple curse word with the permission to struggle that is all we need. Right alongside, the reminder to focus on what is in our control and to choose the joy in the dark hard.

This is the Complicated Gray. The dark and the light. The anger and the acceptance. The longing and the joy. The grief and the peace.

I have no doubt she is with our Savior. She is in no pain, and she is eating her absolute favorite meal with no difficulty or damn spit cup. And, despite the glorious clarity, we will all have when we meet our Savior, I also have no doubt she may be asking Him the questions we had for Him here on earth and in my office.

And still, I want her here changing the world and making all of our lives better and brighter.

The grief and the peace, the damn Complicated Gray.

She thinks I helped and changed her.
She changed me.

God – 21

Justine – 4

She's at peace with Jesus, the world better for knowing her, and still, I miss her so.

The prophecies are fulfilled:
He will wipe away every tear from
their eyes.[a]
Death will be no more;
Mourning no more, crying no more,
pain no more,
For the first things have gone away.
Revelation 21:4

Chapter 24

Oh shit. Shit! Today is child's dedication.

The auditorium was full, just like every other Sunday. The dimmed lights allowed people to close their eyes or lift their hands to the sky or cry tears of joy and/or pain while singing the songs of worship. It is my favorite part of church, and this weekend we were seated towards the front to fill an empty row for the live stream service.

The lights began to brighten after only one song, and immediately the anxiety started to bubble up inside of me as I remembered walking by a bunch of seats marked "Reserved for families of child dedication."

Oh shit. Shit! Today is child's dedication.

Our pastor walked out with his usual kind smile, "Please have a seat," he said. Chad and I took our seats with Mom and Dad next to us just as the line of families filed into the auditorium.

Okay, I can do this. I can focus on how cute the kids are, and I can celebrate through my jealousy. I do not have to get sad.

Couples with children ages birth to three years old, the perfect families stood in front of us asking for the church's support in faithfully raising their children.

Quite literally, the stab in the back, every time it catches me off guard.

I am in what has become my safe place facing what I will never ever have; 2.5 kids, the perfect little family.

Pastor Greg walked down the line saying each child's name out loud. I felt okay at first because the kids are so adorable, some antsy, some in stoic overwhelm of being in front of the crowd, but all adorable. I quickly felt the shift as grief and cynicism bubbled up. I am quickly frustrated at how immediately I began to analyze the group of people at the front.

They seem older. I wonder if they struggled?

Twins. Wonder if they had to do IVF?

That is a big gap between siblings, maybe they struggled? I wonder if they suffered a loss.

What is wrong with me?

But I already know this is what infertility and loss do to you. You almost never can look at a family without wondering if you are coming into contact with a fellow warrior.

1. Because it is so common.
2. Because you want so badly to be around someone who gets it.

"I would like all of the friends and family who have come to support these children and their parents in raising their children with Christ to come up. Please gather around your loved ones as we all, as a congregation, pray over you," Pastor Greg said.

In the darkness of my closed eyes and bowed head, as I attempted to simply focus on Greg's words, the knot in my throat cannot be swallowed down any longer. My next inhale caught as a sob escaped my lips and the tears began to flow. Before I realized I would not be able to catch my next sob the lights dimmed quickly and the music surged drowning out the audible sound of my grief.

Instead of singing my heart out, I sat down and attempted to control my sobbing. I could feel Chad's presence next to me, his calm and kind love I know he was trying to force into my soul right. I heard my Mom sniffle further to my right and felt my Dad's hand on my back, to unfortunately only remind me that I will never be able to make them grandparents to my children.

Will I always be the woman sobbing in church on child dedication day?

God – 21

Justine – 5

Grief strikes again.

I admit how broken I am in body and spirit, but God is my strength, and He will be mine forever.
Psalm 73:26

Chapter 25

"The Froelker pollinators."

When your grief and loss involves kids, it means life passes you by per the seasons and holidays. The wonders of who they would have been haunt you the most during those times of summer fun and right into the traditions of Fall.

"What did you order now?" Chad asked in his responsible accountant voice.

We were both standing in the kitchen going through the mail and feeding the dogs after a long day's work for both of us. At least two times a week, I bring a brown box in from the front step.

"I got the dogs Halloween costumes," I replied, and quickly followed up with, "They were super cheap, I promise!"

He did not have a retort to this at first and instead looked straight at me with the knowing look of I-know-this-is-hard-for-you.

Halloween, as with any of the holidays, even the minor Hallmark-card holidays, is tricky for those of us who wanted kids, but can't have them. Our social media walls fill up with pictures of adorable kids in costumes, and we are always reminded (as if we need an outside reminder) of what could have been, but will never be.

"That's adorable!" I post.

"Too cute!" I write in the comments.

"How fun!" I replied.

I genuinely mean it all. I love seeing my loved ones' children fill up my wall with joy, funny dialogues, and cuteness. And yet, it totally picks at the forever longing that is left after failed infertility treatments.

"Look, these are adorable and educational!" I exclaimed to Chad as I opened the packages to show him the new Halloween costumes, a set of monarch wings for Gertie and Gracie and a bumblebee costume for Bosco.

"The Froelker pollinators," Chad replied with authenticity, and yet I know he is slightly entertaining me.

"I guess I want to be able to post costume pictures next year too," I said as the tears stung my eyeballs ever so slightly.

"I know," he said as he forced me into an embrace while we stood at the end of the kitchen counter.

We usually spend Halloween holed up in our basement with the dogs because they tend to make trick or treating more of a pain than a joy. But we always get our fair share of candy from three of our favorite boys. The Porter's are some of our best friends, and like most of our friends, they have three same gender children, and all three are boys. We always make sure to make plans for dinner and games at their house sometime after Halloween, dessert being the three boys' leftover Halloween candy.

We walked into Scott and Allison's house, in its usual state of construction, both of Legos and their incredible do it yourself remodel project. The boys had shown us their newest Lego builds and were now making me taste their Beanboozled

Jelly Bellys – where two jellybeans looked exactly the same, but one is flavored as buttered popcorn and the other vomit.

We sat at the kitchen table, the boys too excited to have their actual rumps in the seats of the chair.

"Which one?" Kyle sputtered out trying to contain his giggles. He reached out his little hands with two identical jellybeans.

"That one," I said pointing to one.

His eyes brightened as the giggles began to escape his mouth.

I placed the jellybean in my mouth and took a slow bite into it only to be overwhelmed by the stench and taste of vomit.

"Oh, my goooosssh!" I screamed as I spit it out on the table.

"Ha, ha, you got throw up!" all three boys screamed and squealed at the top of their lungs while they bounced around the room laughing.

"That is terrible!"

"Okay, which one next?" It's Will's turn this time.

I placed Will's jellybean into my mouth and again sank my teeth into a terrible taste.

"Oh no, it is dog food!" I screamed this time spitting the jellybean across the room.

The boys could hardly contain themselves. My only slightly exaggerated for effect reaction sent them jumping up and down around the kitchen and laughing at the top of their lungs.

Seeing the pure joy on their faces, I get a slight break with at least a couple normal tasting jelly beans. I let them do this to me for about ten minutes.

"Okay, guys, enough with the jelly beans. Give Justine a break. How about you let her have some of your good candy?" their Mom, and my friend, Allison said.

"Show me the stash!" I urged the boys. Between their neighborhood trick or treat, and the school's trunk or treat, the bounty of three adorable and polite boys is no joke. We all dug into the candy picking out our favorites. Allison and I are always fighting over the Twix, even though both of us try to be gluten free for the most part.

"You can't have these," all three boys all said pulling out their full-size candy bars.

Suddenly out of nowhere Sam, the oldest, said, "You don't have your own kids to fetch you Halloween candy, so that is why you have us!"

I glanced over at Allison making eye contact quickly before shifting my gaze back to the three boys.

Oh, it is so much more than candy my child.

God – 22
Justine – 6

I am fully aware of all the goodness I have only because of the story He has written for me, and yet the holidays sometimes feel like salt in the heartbroken soul.

*Even if the fig tree does not blossom
and there are no grapes on the vines,
If the olive trees fail to give fruit
and the fields produce no food,
If the flocks die far from the fold
and there are no cattle in the stalls;
Then I will still rejoice in the Eternal!
I will rejoice in the God who saves me!*

Habakkuk 3:17-18

Chapter 26

Just(ine) Dance

"I can watch Evan for the day," I tell Sam, "I can arrange my clients so I have the day off and can come help with the boys."

"Really? That would be so helpful. My Mom is always helping with them." Sam replied with more relief than surprise.

"Of course! I'd love to spend the day with Evan. I think I'd be scared to have all three by myself for the whole day, honestly, but I can do after school for sure!"

"You would be totally fine with them all. Okay, this is awesome and so helpful, thank you!"

I showed up in the morning at Seth and Sam's for my day with their youngest son Evan; the two oldest are already at school. Evan's bright blue eyes sparkled with excitement.

"What do you want to do today Evan?" I asked him with just as much excitement as his three-year-old bright blue eyes were beaming back at me.

"Just(ine) Dance!"

Of course, he could probably play Just Dance all day long if I let him.

"I hope you are ready. He has been so excited about his day with Justine," Sam said.

"Me too! Let's do a couple of songs before we have to take your Mom to meet her friends," I replied to Evan.

He chose the kid songs, and of course One Direction, and we danced and laughed while his Mom got her stuff together for her weekend girls getaway.

"Be good for Justine," Sam told Evan, "And have so much fun!"

"We will!" We both said in unison.

"Call Seth or me if you need anything."

"I will don't worry," I said trying to conceal the slightest fear in my voice.

I got back in my car, the exact opposite of a Mom minivan, and turned around to look at Evan. "Ready to go ride the carousel and see the butterflies?' I asked him.

Naturally, I will take any chance to go to The Butterfly House, and having a child with me is the perfect excuse!

"Yes!"

"I want the dragon!" Evan said while running onto the carousel.

"I don't think that one goes up and down, buddy. How about this one?"

"Yea!"

I picked him up and put him on the horse that is already taller than me and made sure the strap was secure around him. "Smile!" I said as I take a selfie.

Our ride circled around for about 3 minutes, both Evan and I smiled the whole time.

"Ready to go see the butterflies!"

Like he has a choice.

"It's hot!" captain obvious Evan screamed as we walked into the glass enclosure full of hot humidity.

"I know! It is because the butterflies live here."

We walked through the butterfly house, me taking pictures both of him and of the gorgeous creatures that bring me closer to God and therefore closer to my three babies.

"Evan, look at me!" I directed him in hopes of getting at least one good shot of him and a butterfly. All of sudden he realized he is much too close to the bright-winged bug and he jumped back.

"Bud, they won't hurt you! They can't even bite you; their mouth is a straw."

"Na uh," he said challenging my butterfly knowledge and stepping even further away out of my photo frame. I can tell his interest is beginning to fade.

"Want to go look at the bugs again?" I asked him referring to the glass enclosures of disgusting bugs in the hallway.

"Yes."

We walked back out to the less humid area where all the bugs and the gift shop are.

"Where is it? What is it?" Evan asked so fast that he is stumbling over his excited questions.

"Can you see it?" I asked him.

"No, I'm too short."

I picked him up at every window so he can find the insect. "What is it?" he asked at every window to which I read him the informative sign and the fun fact.

"I'm hungry," he suddenly stated.

"Okay, where should we go buddy?" Earlier he said he only wanted Chik-Fil-A, "You still want Chick-Fil-A?"

He shook his head, "No!"

"Red Robin, Spaghetti Factory, Chik-Fil-A?" I attempted to list every kid-friendly chain that Chad and I usually try to avoid.

"Buffalo Wild Wings!" Evan blurted out.

"What? Buffalo Wild Wings? Really? Okay"

We hold hands as we walked back to the car in the brisk air. He climbed into his car seat in my college Sentra, and I made sure to fasten his car seat belt correctly. "Okay, Buffalo Wild Wings here we come!" I said with a smile and a kiss on his face.

"NO!"

"Okay well, what then?"

"Red Robin."

"You got it."

We headed to Red Robin, and Evan grabbed his balloon right away. Not knowing protocol I said, "Wait can you just take it like that?" I asked him and the invisible staff not greeting us at the door.

What is kiddo protocol here?

"Yea!"

He climbed up into the booth and decided he wanted chicken strips. I asked him to tell the waitress what he wants. "Quit squirming so much, you're going to fall out of the booth," I said to him once I noticed how high up we are and how close he was to the edge of the seat.

"I want to see the dogs," He said referring to pictures and videos I have on my phone.

He entertained himself on my phone by scrolling through my videos and pictures. Just as I glanced down, I heard the thud and the cry at the same moment, only to see Evan in a pile on the hard tile floor in the middle of Red Robin.

My stomach turned, and I rushed out of the booth to see how hurt he is. I picked him up and put him on my lap.

"You okay?" I asked while I feel around to see if there is a noticeable injury just as I always do with the dogs.

That's what Moms do right?

His tears were crocodile sized, and he feels warm as his body heats up quickly with upset, "My stomach."

We cuddled up for a bit, he stopped crying right as his food came out.

"Feel okay to eat?"

"Yea."

Just then his Dad Seth called on my phone.

"Hey, Seth!"

"Hi, just checking in and wanted to let you know my flight is on time," He told me.

"We're good, just got our food at Red Robin. Here, I'll let you talk to Evan." I replied.

"Red Robin is a good kid day!" I handed off the phone to Evan as if proving he is still alive and well to his Dad and perhaps myself.

"Hi, Daddy!" Evan started babbling to his Dad. "So fun! I fell and hurt myself. I'm okay!"

Oh crap, seriously my first full day by myself and there is an injury!

Evan handed the phone back to me, "Hey! He fell out of the booth and scared me to death!"

"No blood or immediate bruising, no worries!" said the father of three boys who is not easily shaken by injury. "Have fun today! I will see you tonight!"

We headed home after lunch. "What do you want to do dude until your brothers get home from school?"

"Ninja Turtles!" We spent about an hour cuddling on the couch watching cartoon turtles. I can't help but asked him who is who, to which he rolls his eyes but gladly educates me.

"Okay bud, that's enough TV, how about we play some games?" I asserted in my best Mom tone. Mostly because I can tell he is getting antsy and most especially because I cannot take one more minute of those green weird ninja fighting turtles.

We headed upstairs to the playroom loft, and Evan began to pull down multiple games.

Three games of Candyland, a half round of Sorry! and three games of Memory resulted in a victory dance from Evan after overcoming me with seven matches, "Oh yea, oh yea." He sang while dancing in his seat.

"You said you were good at this game."

"Oh yea, a master," He owned.

"Time to head outside and wait for your brothers to get off the bus," I tell Evan. "Let's put all the games away," I instructed him.

"Can I go to my friend's house?" Noah, the oldest yelled, as he and Lane ran off the bus.

"Nope, you're here with me today," I said in the most authoritative motherly voice I can muster.

"Ah man, please?!" Noah grumbled back.

"Nope sorry, we can play games, and your Dad will be home soon anyway."

I let the older boys play their Wii sports games for a bit before I made them choose a game for us all to play together."Can we play Battleship?" Noah asked finally relenting to the fact that he had to hang out with his "Aunt" Justine for at least a few more hours.

"In teams!" I said. "Lane and Noah against Evan and me!"

The little boys made their best effort to whisper what we should hit to Noah and me as we made competitive eye contact over the plastic boards.

"Hit!" I yelled with defeat as Evan rolled over in exasperated joy.

"Yes!" Noah and Lane said in unison.

Seriously, how are they doing that?

"Miiiiisssss!" Noah and Lane sang back at Evan and me. Now Evan rolled over, this time exasperated in disappointment. The giggles getting louder and louder from all three boys.

It is in these times, the pure joy of my chosen children and my engagement with the moment, that if I am not careful can be snatched away so quickly by grief it can send me into instant tears. It is in these times that I breathe. Take a breath in the presence of the joyful moment while also allowing a bit of space to open up for the forever longing I feel for my three. Not necessarily choosing joy over grief, instead making room for both.

God – 23

Justine – 6

*Doing the work to receive the mothering
He has gifted me.*

Hope postponed grieves the heart;
but when a dream comes true, life is full
and sweet.
Proverbs 13:12

Chapter 27

"Want me to put the feather in your hair too?"

"What are you guys doing for Thanksgiving?" I texted Sara, my new friend from church.

"What are you thinking?" She replied quickly.

"Didn't know what or when Matt's family gets together so wanted to welcome you here. I'm cooking Thanksgiving dinner. It will probably just be Chad and me and my parents. We'd love to have you guys too if it works!"

Sara grew up Muslim in Iraq and cannot in contact with most of her family.

"Yes! How about lunch?"

Across the sea of people at our huge church, I made eye contact with her that weekend before service began. She is my new friend. We are still learning a lot from one another but what we both know for sure is that terrible loss has forever changed our lives. We don't compare them, and although very different (mine the loss of three babies and hers the loss of family, and some may said culture) we look at one another with the understanding of our stories being more alike than different.

"Thank you for inviting us."

"Of course!"

"No, thank you. Thank you for getting that I don't have my family really and for getting that it is hard."

"I get it. I get it so much."

The older girls, Kennedy and Emma, walked into the house just as all children always enter the house; scared and yet so excited, mostly because of our three crazy dogs. Most of the kids in our lives have big dogs. And we, well, we are a small dog family. A little dog family with three to be exact.

"Just come in girls, they'll calm down, come in, just push past them," I encouraged them while trying to wrangle the pups.

"Can we try on the costumes now?" Kennedy, the 8-year old said.

"We're going to eat Thanksgiving dinner first. Then we can have our fashion show."

Weeks earlier after realizing I now have three girls in my life that live near me, I had asked Sara if the girls would like my trunk of old dance costumes. "Seriously? They would love that!" She confirmed. Nine years worth of dance costumes, including some dance shoes that had never even been worn before it was all taken away by two back surgeries in high school.

We had one of the most epic Thanksgiving dinners of our life. Chad smoked the turkey, I made the sweet potato casserole, and my Dad made the green bean casserole in the crockpot (read: unhealthy). Both Kennedy and Emma said a prayer of Thanksgiving before we dug in, "Thank you for this food, thank you for Mommy and Daddy, thank you for baby Leah, please keep Mommy's family safe. Amen."

We ate and visited, and I soaked it all in. Kids at my Thanksgiving table eating the food I prepared. Sure, not my kids but some of my new chosen children. Looking around the table at these new friends, I said a quick prayer, *Thank you so much, Lord, thank you.*

"How about dessert?" my Mom asked everyone!

"Yes!" everyone answered back in the Thanksgiving I-am-stuffed-but-still-want-dessert voice we all know.

"We have apple pie! Who wants Cool Whip? Who wants ice cream? And who wants cheese?" she asked.

"Cheese?" Sara asked back very confused.

I smiled back at her, excited to get the reaction I think I will get, "My Dad melts cheese on his apple pie, usually American cheese or Colby Jack. Chad actually likes pepper jack the best."

"What?" Matt, Sara's husband, asked even more confused and now looking at Sara in disgusted disbelief.

"Oh come on, at least try it," I said. "I mean, you always said you grew up eating dirt. This can't be any worse can it?"

"Oh, I'll try it," She responded right away.

"Matt, what about you?" my Mom asked.

"I don't know," He said looking more and more concerned.

"Oh come, you always try things," Sara encouraged him.

My Mom and Dad prepared the smallest bite of warm apple pie with melted cheese for them on one small salad plate and puts it between Sara and Matt. Both sets of eyes shot down to what has now become the dreaded bite of Thanksgiving dessert.

"Just try it," I said.

My famous words. My Mom is notoriously a very simple eater. Common comments at our dinner table are, "Your plate is literally all brown." Or "Just try it."

Sara carefully sliced the tiny bite in half and placed the fork into her mouth slowly. As she chewed, her face softened just a bit realizing that it maybe is not so bad.

"It's okay. I don't think I like the texture," she said, "Come on Matt." Matt's eyes have not moved from the bite of pie, and his face has only continued to scrunch into a facial expression of more disgust. Sara's eyes lit up a bit, "I've never seen him like this, he's always willing to try anything."

By then, Kennedy and Emma and I were giggling, and my Mom and Dad were encouraging him, "Come on Matt, just try it."

Matt placed the fork in his mouth and began to chew as his face did not soften at all like Sara's did but slightly twisted with even more disgust. "That's terrible," He stated.

And, with that dinner was over.

Everyone laughed and giggled. It only got quiet when the girls realized that dinner is over, "Can we try on the costumes now?"

After cleaning up we all headed down to the basement, I told everyone to sit around our sectional as I headed to the unfinished part of the basement for my massive dance trunk. Kennedy's eyes lit up at the site of the size and my struggle to bring it in. Emma looked to her sister for how she should be reacting.

I opened the trunk to reveal the bright colors, sequins, and tutus. Their two little bodies propelled themselves forward almost landing entirely inside the trunk.

"Girls, back up. Let Justine pull out the costumes for you," Sara said laughing.

Mom and Dad sat next to her holding baby Leah. I stole a glance at them smiling at her and glancing at the two older girls.

I felt a tug at my heart for a second.

There is no doubt they dreamed of watching their grand-daughters try on these costumes. The costumes they sacrificed so much time and money for as I was growing up.

I pulled out two costumes at a time, and asked the girls which ones they wanted to try on.

They tried on all of them!

Every single one of them, despite whether they fit or not.

"Ooh, I love this one!" Kennedy said her voice full of wonder.

Emma walked out with an emerald green tap leotard costume on, an excellent choice considering it has both sequins and feathers on it. In her young age, she had put both legs through one leg hole. We all laughed, and I helped her adjust.

"Want me to put the feather in your hair too?" I asked her.

"Yes!" her eyes got even bigger. I clipped the green feathers into her long dark curly hair.

"Shall we finish it off with the shoes too?"

"Yessss," eyes even bigger.

I helped her into the gold spray-painted high healed tap shoes that are much too big for her tiny feet.

"Okay, can you show us your dance moves?"

Emma moved her feet and wiggled her hips while placing her arms above her head like she has seen Princess Elsa in *Frozen* do many times over.

Everyone had smiles on their faces.

It is a full circle kind of moment for me, the costumes I've held onto my whole adult life, moving them from house to house, all with the dream and expectation that my girls would be playing dress up in them.

God had other plans.

Still, it is one of the best moments of my child*full* life.

God – 24

Justine – 6

Two families that aren't family, who have become family, all through Christ.

give thanks to God no matter what circumstances you find yourself in. (This is God's will for all of you in Jesus the Anointed.)
1 Thessalonians 5:18

Chapter 28

"We have a heart!"

Between clients I got the text from Chad, "Mom and Dad asked me to come out to Colorado."

"Of course! Do you need me to cancel my clients, do you need me there?" I replied.

"I don't think so."

"Are you sure?"

"I don't know."

"Okay, I need you to asked Josh how serious this is and asked him if we both need to be there. Okay?"

"Okay."

It is Monday after Thanksgiving and Chad's sister, Becky, has experienced a Spontaneous Coronary Arterial Dissection at the age of 34 years old, basically a massive heart attack, despite being incredibly athletic and healthy. There have been a lot of scary updates since Friday when Becky was taken in for chest pains. Chad's family can be pretty non-communicative at times, and it was hard to tell how serious this was from across the country as they were in Colorado for the holiday and we were still home in Saint Louis. Thank God we had Josh, Chad's friend from college who is also an excellent cardiologist.

"He said we both need to go now," Chad replied much quicker than I expect.

Clients canceled, the very early morning flight booked and no sleep at all, and we are standing at the airline counter asking if we can sit together. My stomach turns, and I get really hot as the tears sting my eyes, "You okay?" Chad asked.

"I think I'm having a PTSD flashback. We just did this nine months ago for Dad," I replied trying to hold it together in front of the TSA workers.

"I know."

Nine months prior we stood at a similar counter in Vegas trying to get home to make a four-hour trip car drive to Iowa after getting word that my Dad had fallen 6 feet off a ladder hitting every rung on the way down to only rest with his forehead on the core drill bit.

Nine months prior we hadn't gotten any sleep as we waited for updates from the hospital and anticipated an earlier than the butt crack of dawn alarm to catch our flight.

Nine months prior we had no idea if my Dad would be okay, let alone live.

And here we were now, doing the same thing for Chad's sister.

Why was this happening again?

How could this be happening again?

How dare this freaking happen again!

We arrived at the hospital to find Chad and Becky's parents, Jim and Terry, and Becky's husband, Jeremiah exhausted from waiting up all night for Becky to be taken into surgery for a clot developing in her left ventricle. She was finally taken back that afternoon.

"We all need to sleep, especially you three," I begin bossing everyone around like a pushy mother. I boss because I wish I would have had someone doing that for me when my Dad fell. "Yes…" is mumbled by all three of them.

We gather pillows and blankets from the staff at the hospital which includes my college friend and sorority sister Ashley who works just down the hall from the waiting room we will be living in for the next however many weeks.

Several hours passed and we are all woken up by the doctors and the cricks in our bodies from sleeping on the hard floor or uncomfortable hospital chairs. "The clot has been removed, and we have placed Becky on ECMO," her surgeon explains, I don't even know how many hours later. Becky's heart at this point is dead and no longer working. The ECMO will serve as her heart pumping and oxygenate her blood through her system until she gets a new heart.

She's alive but needs a new heart and won't leave the hospital until she gets it.

"Go to the hotel and get some real sleep. You need your strength for the long road ahead," the surgeon ordered us.

Like zombies, we head across the street to the hotel where we are all sharing a room for the next couple of nights at least.

"I don't have pajama bottoms, I always just sleep in my shirt and underwear," my mother-in-law Terry said with slight embarrassment in her voice.

"Well, I've had two back surgeries in high school where rooms of people would see me naked. And I taught Human Sexuality for a few years, so it doesn't bother me! We know you have a butt and legs, just get in bed real fast," I said trying to lighten the mood some because I know how healing laughter can be in times of trauma. I've survived more than one of them for God's sake.

"I won't look, I promise," Chad said with all seriousness and yet his usual deadpan humor.

We all slept for a good five or six hours that night in real beds and with real pillows. Now it was time for five people to shower and head to the hospital. As I finished at least making my hair presentable, Terry came out of the bathroom, "I've never used shampoo and conditioner like that before. It smells so good too." She moved her head about as if to allow her short hair to flow in the self-made wind.

"What do you mean?" I asked. Chad and Jim are both ignoring us at this point.

"It was like a scrub. I've never seen shampoo like that. But my hair smells so nice and feels great."

"Wait, which bottles did you use?" I asked, beginning to see that we may have a pretty funny situation on our hands.

"Just the hotel ones."

"Me too but there wasn't any scrub... Oh my gosh! Chad!" I squealed with laughter realizing what she had done.

"What?" both Terry and Chad replied.

"Did you use these?" I asked Terry holding up what are two matching bottles from a hotel, however not our current hotel, which said shampoo and conditioner on them.

"Yes! Smell them; they smell so good!" Terry said still in the afterglow of her spa-like experience using scrub shampoo and conditioner.

"These are a body scrub and a facial scrub Chad just happened to put into old matching hotel shampoo and conditioner bottles," I said no longer containing my laughter.

"What? You mean I washed my hair with a facial scrub?"

"Yes," I giggled.

"Well, my hair has never looked better!"

"We have our million dollar idea!" I exclaimed.

Back at the hospital, we learned Becky's chest cavity was filling with fluid, and they needed to take her back into the OR to see where the bleed is. She was now officially on the top of the transplant list for a new heart. Waiting for an OR and surgeon to become available Becky became more and more uncomfortable as her chest filled with more and more fluid.

"This is urgent but not an emergency," her nurses explained to us as our worry and frustration grew.

A bedside procedure to drain the fluid seemed to be only a temporary fix.

Finally, Becky was taken back as we are all left to attempt to rest on the hospital floor. A couple of hours later Becky's surgeon nudged us all into coherence and said, "We found a small bleed, her chest cavity is dry. She's already fighting the tube. Go said hi but then you all need to go to the hotel and get some sleep."

Once again Becky was responsive and fighting the tube. Once extubated her first words were no match for all the machines beeping around her, "You need to pray over me."

The six of us grabbed one another's' hands and my father-in-law prayed, "Lord, thank you for keeping Becky safe through this procedure. Thank you for her doctors. Please continue to be with us all through this and heal Becky."

With that, we all said goodnight and left for the hotel to try to sleep.

The next morning we were greeted with a groundhog's day of sorts. Becky's chest cavity is filling with fluid again, and she would need to be taken back into the OR. "Same thing as last night. We'll go in, find the bleed, patch it up and continue to wait for the new heart," her surgeon reports.

Those of us who could attempted to do some work on our phones and computers. Jim made phone calls to family back home. And, Terry talked. Because that is what she does best, God love her she must fill any empty space with her voice.

"I'm going to go walk my prayer hall," she announced to all of us in the waiting room. Just a few yards from what had become our home in the cardiac waiting room was a long hall Terry had taken to pacing and praying out loud in.

"Want company?" I asked her.

"Yes," she replied.

We linked arms and slowly pace the long hall back and forth.

"Pastor said I could beg God to save her."

"Absolutely, you can," I agreed with her.

"We can still trust God's will and asked for what we want."

"I sure hope so," I said back to her with questioning humor in my voice.

We walked together losing track of time as we both silently and audibly pleaded with God, and comforted one another. Later as we sit in the waiting room chairs in silence, she asked me, "Is it different this time? Your faith is so much stronger now than when your Dad fell, does it feel different?"

"It does. Despite everything, there is still a sense of trust. He's got this, He's got her," I replied back while knowing for one of the first times in my life I never believed those words more.

"She's stable," Becky's surgeon reported after a much longer than anticipated operation. "We've removed the ECMO and placed her on a RVAD and LVAD, pumps for both sides of her heart until a donor's heart matches."

"Thank God," We all said aloud. "Thank you."

"Now we wait for her new heart."

After a few days of Becky being stable Chad and I head back home to Saint Louis. There is not much for us to do at the hospital while we wait for a donor's heart. The crew back in Colorado would send us daily updates so that I could update the CaringBridge website for everyone. It was my way to help, writing had become a true love for me and updating everyone via a blog dedicated to Becky's progress took quite a bit of stress off everyone.

For 13 days Chad and I jumped quickly every time the phone rang hoping it was that call telling us to get on the next flight because Becky had a heart.

"It's so hard. We are praying for someone to lose their life so Becky can live. It's awful and amazing all at the same time," I said to Chad one night in bed.

"I know, one family's loss for another family's miracle, the Complicated Gray," he said with a wink.

I had already seen four clients with three left to go when I saw my phone light up with my in-law's name and number. I answered before the first ring even finished.

"Hey, everything ok?" I nearly shouted.

"We have a heart!" my mother in law Terry exclaimed.

"Really?! Thank God!"

"We don't know much, just that it is in Kansas City. We don't even know yet when the doctors will fly out to get it. Still, have a lot of hurdles, but we have a heart!"

"Oh my gosh, I will get a hold of Chad and start looking at flights right now! Let us know if anything changes. We love you all!"

I called, texted and emailed Chad at work, "They have a heart!!"

Chad called me back, "What do we know?"

"Not much besides it is in Kansas City. They still have to get it out and inspect it and make sure it is good enough for her. The heart is the last organ harvested."

"So we need to fly out when?"

"Tomorrow. Can you book the flight so I can get texts out to my clients canceling and get myself together for the next few clients I need to see tonight?"

"Yep, love you. See you when you get home."

I took a deep breath and prayed out loud as if to make sure He hears me, "Please God help me to be present during these sessions. Help me to provide the care these clients need and deserve. Please continue to keep Becky stable. And please, please God be with the family who just lost their loved one."

"She's getting a Missouri heart!" Terry nearly squealed.

"Let's hope she doesn't all of a sudden start liking Jayhawk blue because then we know the heart is from the wrong side of Kansas City," Chad joked back referring to the entire family's love for the Mizzou Tigers, whose colors are black and gold.

The day was spent waiting for the doctors to fly out to Kansas City to get the heart. Before we knew it, Becky was back in surgery, and all of us were in the Lord's hands. Much sooner than anyone expected her surgeons came out and sat in the waiting room among all of us.

"The heart is in. It is the perfect size, young and healthy. It even beat on its own. The next six days are critical. But from what she has shown us, we expect her to do well."

The only words possible to utter, "Thank you, thank you."

The very next day the most spoken words, by Becky, herself, "I got a new heart!" She would said it to everyone who came into her room with a light and joy that only a new lease on life can give. Just 24 hours or so after receiving her new heart Becky was out of bed and taking a few steps to a chair to eat dinner. It took a team to get her those few steps but together we witness the beginning of her new life.

Day 3 with her new heart we hung out and cared for her. "Ready to try a walk down the hall?" her nurse said as she came in the room.

"Really?" all of us said in unison. Chad, his parents and I were reading and chatting on and off while Becky rested throughout the morning.

"Yep, we want to get her moving and make that heart work," the nurse said, "the sooner, the better."

With medical staff in front of her and behind her Becky's pale hands hold the walker as she takes her first steps out of her room with her new heart. Jim and Terry both with tears in their eyes stay along the wall while Chad pushed a machine and I, of course, took a video.

"Look at you!"

"Walking with a brand new heart!"

"Thank God!"

With a glimmer in her eye she took her hands off the walker for a split second, "Look no hands!" She walked most of the length of the ICU unit that first walk. And in proud awe, we got to witness it.

A true miracle.

Later, after the tough walk down the hall, we have a spa day. Chad, Terry, a nurse and I washed Becky's hair together. And then I spent quite a while brushing through it since it hadn't been cared for in weeks, a beating heart is much more critical. As I piled her hair on top of her head into a messy bun, I asked her, "Want to see? It's much better and has to feel better I hope."

"Thank you," she responded while grabbing my hand.

We make eye contact like we never have before, "You're welcome."

That night we all tag teamed helping her eat a cup of broccoli cheddar soup. Took us trying three different spoons and a lot of coaching but she was able to get some soup in her belly. After all of the tubes, eating or swallowing all of her new pills would be something that would not come easy for quite a while.

After a couple of days and Becky's continued improvement, it was time for Chad and me to said see you later and head back to Saint Louis again. This time not knowing when we would be back made it very hard. That evening Chad and I walked to grab everyone dinner and sat down with just Becky to eat. It was the first time since I have known her in ten years that we had really had an authentic conversation outside of small talk.

"You deserve more than you believe. My hope and prayer is that through this you finally see it," I told her.

Her eyes begin to well with tears, and she shifts her focus back down to her broccoli cheddar soup.

I continued, "Thank you for allowing me to help, thank you for allowing me to mother in many ways. I will be forever grateful to you for it."

She shook as she hugged me tight despite just getting a new heart. Unable to said any other words she only muttered, "Thank you for everything."

God – 25

Justine – 6

*I'm realizing He's there, right beside me,
even in the anger and fear.*

I tell you the truth: whoever believes in Me
will be able to do what I have done, but
they will do even greater things, because
I will return to be with the Father. 13
Whatever you ask for in My name, I will do it
so that the Father will get glory from the Son.
14 Let Me say it again: if you ask for anything in My name, I will do it.
John 14:12-14

Chapter 29

The silence of your life gone too soon.

"We'd like you to speak at our Angel of Hope Ceremony if you would?" Debbie, Executive Director of Share Pregnancy and Infant Loss Support, said.

"Really?" I replied with a bit of shock.

I remain in shock that Share lets me be such a part of their organization. I know this is shame talking though, it's attempt to steal my light like a dementor in the Harry Potter series.

The shame that I didn't try long or hard enough for my babies.

The shame that mine were only embryos.

The shame of this journey that tells me I am not enough because I am not a mother.

Through my work, I know better, yet that doesn't mean shame is gone forever.

On a chilly December night, I read a poem I wrote in front of hundreds of families holding white flowers and candles. Many of them were there as a tradition to honor their lost babies with their families by listening to a few poems be read and laying white flowers at the foot of the Angel of Hope. The families then could be seen walking along the brick paths stopping to have a moment over a brick that is engraved with their child's name.

There are too many of them.

Chad and I walked them together as we waited for people to arrive; him being the supportive husband and business manager and me attempting to calm my nerves about speaking in front of this many people, especially with shame nipping at my worthiness.

I take a deep breath as she introduces me to the podium, *loss is loss*.

And I speak the words I hope will provide comfort and knowing for the all parents of angels in front of me:

The darkness left behind by the loss of you
can feel as if the breath,
the very essence of who we once were
and who we wanted to be,
has been taken from us.

Some days the darkness so heavy it can be challenging to put one foot in front of the other,
let alone breathe.
Some days the dawn strikes
and our love for you fills us with wonder so powerful it propels us forward
in the day of the living.

The wonder of how your giggles
would have filled our souls with joy,

instead allowing our hearts to hear for us in the silence that
can stifle us.
The silence of your life gone too soon
scarring our souls,
trusting we always know and see you
as our hearts will forever speak you.

Missing the warmth of your skin in our arms
and yet, we feel you
holy every day and always.

Never to know the tangible completeness
always wondering who you might have been
and who we could have been.

And yet, trusting and knowing we are whole,
even in our endless longing.

We will spend the rest of our lives moving through the grief
with whatever grace we can muster in that day.
Choosing to give ourselves graceful permission to embrace
the paradox that is defining our happy ending
within the arms of lifelong loss.

Within these arms of permission
and unwavering hope we can find our truth.

Our truth to live our lives in pure honor of you.

Because through this honor we fight,
fight to take back the pieces of ourselves
that grief has tried to plunder from our souls.
Taking back the pieces of you in us
battling to weave them into the fabric
of what we must carry with us always.

The battle of who we once were
and who we are now
as we parent you from afar.
Parenting with scarred souls
the scars which were once shattered hearts
through which we are forever changed.

Forever changed
and yet choosing to be always healing.

Healing within the Complicated Gray
of our eternal love for you and the darkness of grief.

In the tension of sorrow and love,
walking into this Complicated Gray
awakening to life in color
we breathe glory into our lives.

The glory of our love for you.
The glory of you.

God – 26

Justine – 6

Honoring my three always, who were never really mine to begin with.

Every bird flying over the mountains I know; every animal roaming over the fields belongs to Me.
Psalm 50:11

Chapter 30

"We have our own Christmas tradition."

They would have been three. Old enough to get the whole Santa thing. Old enough that we would have baked cookies for Santa, left treats for his reindeer and been exhausted as parents with three-year-olds at Christmas.

But they aren't here.

It is sad.

And yet, I am okay.

The few weeks leading up to the holidays included one of our due dates. December 21st, just four days shy of Christmas, was the date our last embryo, our last shot at having children was to be born had IVF worked. That Monday passed like any other, taking care of myself and seeing several clients. The weeks between Thanksgiving and Christmas are filled with holiday parties, shopping and trying my best to manage the feelings that come with holiday cards that arrived in the mail.

"Oh, that is so cute!" I said out loud more to myself than to Chad.

"Who's is that?" Chad asked taking the card next examining it for the cuteness I have proclaimed.

"Caroline and Steve's," I replied, "What a cute way to announce they are pregnant."

It doesn't sting with people I love most. But the combination of the due date and the holidays makes the word pregnant hang in my throat longer than I expect.

"That is cute," Chad said.

We have discussed how much more straightforward this journey is for him as a guy. Once after a big event at church, I asked him, "Does it ever bother you that we, a couple like us who can't have kids, are never mentioned or even thought about?'

"Not really," He replied simply which seemed only to cut my pain deeper.

"How often do you think about it or even them?" I asked him referring to our babies.

"Not near as often as I know you do. But I think it is because I am a guy."

"Because of how you are wired?" I asked, confused.

"Babe, guys don't stand around and talk about their kids. We talk about work, sports and sometimes cars. Kids are hardly ever, ever brought up."

"And most of the time, kids are the only thing women do talk about," I said with frustrated clarity.

I finish going through the cards and pick up ours. That year, the year they would have been three, the front side has my usual hysterical and adorable pictures of the dogs. The other side had a family portrait of Chad and me with shadows of the three kids.

"Doing okay?" Chad asked as he puts his hands around me.

"I am sadder this year than I expected."

"Why do you think that is?"

"They would have been three this year. Christmas is so fun with the magical, and crazy, mind of a three-year-old."

"I know," He said hugging me tighter.

For that moment, I allowed the tears to fall down my face.

Though the sadness surprised me that year I made sure to build in a lot of joy that Christmas. Chad, Mom, Dad and I spent most of the day Christmas Eve at church serving; Mom, Dad and I served in the nursery and Chad parked cars. After our second service of serving Dad rushed to get in line for good seats in the auditorium. Our church will see over 20,000 people between all three of our locations; it is epic, to said the least.

Mom and I finished up in the nursery and find Chad and meet Dad in line.

"I know exactly what you are going to said, but I still can't believe it," Dad said while we are standing in the crowded lobby of the church.

"Said it anyway," I replied to him.

"I mean, it is Christmas. And that Dad dropped off his daughter wearing jeans and a hoodie. It's Christmas. But I already know what you are going to said."

"And what's that?" I smiled back at him.

"God doesn't care about what we wear on the outside; he cares about what is in our hearts."

"Yep! Isn't it amazing?" I exclaimed back at him with a wink.

Together we sit through a magical service. The couple without kids for Christmas. On our way out the door, I saw Sara working security. "Merry Christmas!" we both said at the same time as we hug one another.

"What are you guys doing tonight? Come over?" She asked.

"Sorry, we can't. We have our own Christmas tradition. We go out to a nice dinner, drink a bottle of wine and hang out on Christmas Eve."

"I want to drink wine," She said meaning so well, I love her so much more.

Part of me wants to replied, "I want a three-year-old to put to bed tonight dreaming of Santa." Instead, I said, "Text me, and we can figure something out. We need to bring the girls their gift. Merry Christmas."

And with the freedom that a child*full* life provides, we went to dinner at our favorite restaurant for our Christmas Eve. When we got home, we open gifts with Mom and Dad and headed to bed.

Our traditions continue Christmas morning with a delicious, not so good for you, breakfast with Mom and Dad before they head to my grandma's. After Mom and Dad hit the road Chad and I made the rounds. First stop is to see Noah, Lane, and Evan. We love to have Santa show and tell on Christmas morning. There is nothing quite like a child showing off their new finds that Santa brought.

"Merry Christmas!" We shouted as we walk into Seth and Sam's house.

"Merry Christmas!" Everyone shouted back.

"We're going to Disney World!" Evan yelled at the top of his lungs.

"I heard! Are you so excited?" I said back.

And all at once the three boys start spouting off what their favorite part of their trip will be. "We leave tomorrow!" Evan shouted through hurt your gut laughter.

We eat together and visit with Evan interrupting every so often with, "Can we open our presents?"

We rally all of them together, "You have to open them together this year boys," I instructed. I knew about the trip, and Sam asked me to see if there was anything that could go along with it this year. So I settled on personalized bags and autograph books.

"A book?" Noah opened it a bit confused.

"It is so you can get all the autographs of the princesses and Mickey and everyone!" I explain hoping they would be excited.

Noah's eyes light up unexpectedly, he is the oldest, I wasn't sure if he would be into it. His Mom goes on, "When we meet everyone you can asked them to sign your book!"

"Cool!" I get with the little kid validation that means more to me than anyone will probably ever truly understand.

Next stop is the Porter's, quite possibly the easiest family we have in our lives to purchase gifts for, as you cannot go wrong with Legos. We had warned all of our chosen families that instead of three gifts (one for each boy) we were doing family gifts in observance of Advent Conspiracy. This year we were spending less money, spending more time relationally, giving more and worshipping fully. And with the grace and love I knew they have for us, all of our friends understood entirely.

We walked into the Porter's house, and I'm reminded of my Christmases growing up; toys everywhere and sporting the PJs still in the late afternoon.

Sam, the oldest, is at the dining room table building his new Lego set with the concentration of a rocket scientist. "Hi, Sam!" I said.

"Hi! Merry Christmas!"

Will stood up and pointed down at his contraption on the floor, "Look!" He is always the one that wants to show and explain things to us.

And Kyle is running around with his hands in everything as usual.

We visited for a while with Scott and Allison and laugh with the kids.

"Want to open your gift boys?" I asked.

"Yes!" they all said together.

"I bet it is Legos," Sam said.

"How do you know?" I wink back at him.

They tear it open together, and I get major points for finding a set with a Lego brick that lights up.

"It is the only one we can put together in the dark!" Will exclaimed.

"Thank you!" They all said in unison with only the slightest prompt from their Mom Allison.

Chad and I headed home for dinner with his parents at our house and to open gifts. A Christmas without children when you wanted them will never be without longing. So every year

I will take that longing, and honor my babies, and love the children who are in my life.

God – 27

Justine – 6

It doesn't seem to get better. Just different.

Into the home of the childless bride,
He sends children who are, for her, a cause
of happiness beyond measure.
Praise the Eternal!
Psalms 113:9

Chapter 31

"Oh no, he isn't mine."

"McKinley, you want to color with me this morning?" I asked the sleepy-eyed almost three-year-old. We arrived last night for our annual trip to Las Vegas to see our goddaughter McKinley and meet her new baby brother Ben.

"Color?" She said looking confused as she knows it is actually breakfast time.

"Aunt Justine colors in the morning McKinley," Her Mom Casey said in full support even though I know a part of her thinks, and knows I believe in and do some weird stuff. Casey was my college roommate and still one of my best friends. Our personalities always more complimentary than similar, Casey has always been by my side.

"Go show Aunt Justine where your colors are," Casey told McKinley.

"Come on!" McKinley said as she grabs my hand and pulls me towards the guest bedroom where we are staying for the weekend. I grabbed the ultra washable markers and one coloring book.

I put McKinley in her booster seat at the kitchen island. I sat next to her with my Johanna Basford adult coloring book page that I traveled with and the handful of colored pencils and markers I packed. Side by side we ate breakfast and colored together. McKinley stole some of my fruit and decides my coloring book page would be prettier with stickers on it.

"McKinley color on your own, Aunt Justine's is pretty," Casey redirected her.

"It's okay. We can make it even prettier with stickers," I smiled at McKinley as she giggled and slapped another sticker right over top my newly colored flower.

"It's beautiful!" I said with complete joyful love like I am not sure I have ever felt.

There she was, our goddaughter, who we only get to see a couple of times a year if we are lucky, coloring with me. No other words worthy of uttering than, thank you.

A germ infested warehouse full of fun and filled with bigger than life rainbow colored bounce houses, and we have the place almost to ourselves!

A child's favorite place to bounce as high as they can for stomach dropping fun.

A parent's place of refuge to run some energy out of them.

An infertile couples' worst nightmare.

The hum coming from the blowers filled the soft structures to the ceiling provided an undercurrent of white noise to the giggles and happy squeals coming from the two other children who are already there with their Mom. Baby Ben was asleep in his car seat content for the time being. McKinley kicked off her Crocs, Chad untied his shoes, and I unzipped my boots racing to see whose stocking feet can hit the bright red vinyl floor of the first bounce house. We both ran after McKinley as she hurled her tiny, not quite three-year-old self into the soft and bouncy structure.

"Wait for us!" I yelled at her, already immersed in breathless excitement.

All I could hear were her giggles. I immediately felt off balance as I entered the first bounce house, my experience with them not near that of the three-year-old I am who is with me. I bounced off the side a few times before I had my bearings enough to climb after McKinley as she attempted to scale a wall that is way too big for her.

Her smile and laughter burst brighter than the colored vinyl world we are stumbling in. She flung her body in complete abandonment, jumping for joy so high that we are left with no other option but for our faces to cramp from smiling so much. For an hour we trailed behind her playing. Helping her up the ladders or climbing walls that are a smidge too big for her tiny arms and legs.

"Hold onto the straps so you can pull yourself up," I instructed her.

"Come on McKinley. You can do it!" Chad said looking down at her from the top already.

"Okay," she quietly assured me with a nod of her tiny head and immediately grabbed the strap.

This smallest teaching seems to light a spark under her as she then raced up the ladder at double the speed. My knees ached as I try to catch up to her.

All three of us perched precariously at the top of a slide that was much bigger than I anticipated, as McKinley shouted, "Race!"

My stomach dropped with surprise at the steepness of the slide and a laugh escaped my smile so loud I even startle myself.

"Again, again!" McKinley shouted.

"Okay!" I shouted back in a funny voice much to her delight!

"MYself," she stated back brimming with threenager attitude.

This time I waited for her at the bottom. Her blonde hair sticks straight up as she caught wind on the way down and her face shined with unbridled joy like only a three-year-old can.

We'd been playing for nearly an hour, and my body was beginning to feel it. My legs had started to turn to jelly from all the jumping. I rolled up my sleeves and pulled my long red hair up into a messy bun on top of my head. My thirty-six-year-old bad back was telling me I needed a break, so I go over to the bench where my friend Casey was holding Ben. I took Ben out of her arms with a slight smile and unspoken words of love.

At only eleven weeks old he has the new baby smell that fills your nose with maternal love upon the first breath. His eyes lit up, and he cracked a huge smile imitating back to me my joy in him.

I nuzzled him, smiled at him and felt his warmth in my arms making sure to soak in every scent, smile and snuggle that I can.

After a bit, Casey asked, "Want me to take him back so you can go and play again?"

"I'm good for now," I replied.

"Need a little break, huh?" Casey asked, teasing back as if to said, *we are getting so old, aren't we?*

She's assuming my body needs a break, but it's my heart that needs one too. I glanced back at Chad picking up McKinley to help her make a shot in the basketball bounce house. They were both giggling and jumping everywhere. The thought crept in ever so slightly, just like it usually does.

He would have been a great Dad.

Two back surgeries in high school, which included a year and a half of being misdiagnosed and a year in a body cast, had been the massive wrecking ball to the dream of ever carrying a healthy pregnancy for us.

Five years ago, we began our journey to make our family by posting an ad on a surrogacy website. The ad read, "We are looking for more information on gestational surrogacy. We are at the very beginning of the process and looking for resources and research. Thank you!"

We were inundated with emails from hundreds of women before our hearts chose a first time surrogate and mother of two.

A couple of failed rounds of IVF, tens of thousands of dollars and three lost babies later we ended our journey without the desired, hoped for, dreamed of and paid for outcome of our own children.

In our world's most accepted definition of a parent, we will never meet the criteria. I will never birth a child, and we are not adopting one. Some call us childless. Some will even said that we will never know true love.

To which, I will emphatically and stubbornly correct them and let them know that we are childfull parents, birthing a rare kind of parenthood. As childfull parents we seek out, asked for and remain open enough to receive the gift of being involved in our friends' children's' lives.

It is a gift that has not come without cost and loss.

It is still a gift.

A gift of love.

And love is love, isn't it?

"How old is he?" a very blonde mother asked, interrupting me from my thoughts. I sat down with baby Ben on the unnecessarily uncomfortable bench. I noticed quickly she is playing on her phone while her two kids run and bounce away.

I give myself permission to think the first thought that comes from the bitter infertile part of myself, *Play with your kids lady, you get to have them.* The thought briefly passes through my mind.

I know all too well how little time and care most mothers provide for themselves, especially as a mental health therapist. Most of my work with mothers consists of teaching them how to take better care of themselves, so they don't end back up in my office in their fifties lost and completely empty. I quickly practiced my empathy and thought, *I'm so glad Moms have places like this to entertain their kids a bit so they can get the occasional break.*

"Eleven weeks," I smiled and replied to her question.

"Oh my gosh, you look aaaamaaazing!" she exclaimed.

"Oh, no, he isn't mine. We're in town visiting." I quickly corrected her. I pointed to Casey and said, "This is Mom, my friend, Casey."

"Oh, well, you look great too!"

We all exchanged obligatory smiles as I stood up and walked closer to the bounce houses away from the woman who I assumed will probably asked me any minute where my own kids are.

Justine, don't get sad. Breathe! Stay present.

I stood with baby Ben in my arms, I shifted my focus back to Chad and McKinley bouncing away, as I allowed the sadness to pass through me. Rather, I allowed it to well up as it will always live inside of me. Some days it comes in waves like this, waves of sadness triggered by thoughts like, *It wasn't supposed to be this way*, or *What if...* Other days it is the underlying longing that will never go away as a mother of children who never took a breath of this earth's fresh air.

Always, I acknowledge the thoughts and the feelings, giving myself permission to feel them all. I am simply too afraid not to, because then it is like they never existed, and they are our children. Even if the only thing we have left of them, besides our forever longing hearts and forever changed lives, is a picture from our infertility clinic of their eight-cell embryo beings.

I fought to take a breath and looked down at baby Ben. At eleven weeks, he is a true miracle in my life. I took another breath, deeper and more knowing, and looked back at Chad and McKinley jumping like crazy in the bounce house together. With yet another deeper breath, a space began to open up within me, and the sadness moved just enough to allow space for another choice.

I am so grateful, thank you.

I am grateful for these moments.

I am grateful we were given our babies. I am thankful we were chosen as their parents if only to love them from afar.

Because they are what we have.

And, don't we love what we get at the end of the day?

My love, a love with the endless wonder of who they would have been and who we could have been as parents. A wonder that I must choose, every damn day, in how it defines me for the rest of my life.

The rush of air from McKinley running full force to another bounce house brought my head back to real time. Chad took the baby from me, "Go play for a while," he said as he kisses the top of my head.

"Thank you," I replied allowing him, and only him, to see my eyes glistening with the slightest of tears. I ran to catch McKinley headed up the ladder to the big slide. We reached the top of the slide together. Chad was waiting at the bottom holding one of our many chosen children. I felt the pull of my forever longing and my gratitude, all at the same time. We made eye contact to silently say to one another, "It is okay. We are okay. And this is amazing still."

I held McKinley's hand tight, threw my head back and let laughter escape from my soul, lightening my spirit, as we slid down together one more time.

God – 28

Justine – 6

Her giggle.

*You did it: You turned my deepest pains into
joyful dancing;
You stripped off my dark clothing
and covered me with joyful light.*
Psalm 30:11

Chapter 32

"So I am on my own for the first night?"

When you attend a huge church the only way to make it feel like family is to get involved. I also knew I needed my faith to be more than a 70-minute service on the weekend. Getting my feet wet with serving in the nursery was feeling great. Getting baby time to fill up a piece of my longing soul, while also loving on those kiddos so moms and dads could enjoy the service completely, was terrific. The 5 minutes of pick up time tended to be brutal. My forever scarred heart struggled some days when the little ones ran to the counter screaming, "Mommy!!!"

I will never hear anyone call me mommy.

I feel the pang of grief, take a breath and allow the joy to come in also.

I knew that serving in the nursery alone was not utilizing some of my best gifts, especially my spiritual gifts of mercy and faith. Facilitating *Explorations* was a great start, but I knew I needed to give more of myself. So I signed up for our Quarterlife class. Quarterlife is a class for post college 20-29-year-olds. We cover a topic each semester such as identity, jobs, and relationships. Working with quarterlife clients is one of my favorite demographics so I knew I would love it, but I also knew I had to be very cognizant of being a faith and life mentor and not a therapist. The more involved I become at church, the more aware I must be of that boundary. As much as the therapist part of me is all of me, I cannot be a therapist all of the time to the people in my life. It is not fair to either one of us, plus I do therapy as a job. As in, I like getting paid for it.

My Quartlerlife table happened to include six girls my first semester facilitating it. The first night, as I waited for my seasoned facilitator veteran to show up, it was getting closer and closer to start time. I went to find Pastor Joel, "Um, Ashley is not here yet."

"Okay, let's check around."

After touching base with a few people, we learned that she would not be coming.

"So I am on my own for the first night?" I said to him with fear both in my voice and in my eyes.

"I know you can do it but if you need me just pull me in."

"Okay, I know I can too, just nervous."

As God would have it, my co-facilitator was not there the second week either. To which I let Joel know our group had a dynamic and a trust that was already building.

I think I can do this myself.

And just like that, I was facilitating a class at church on my own.

Who would have ever thought that but God Himself!

God – 29

Justine – 6

Well, dang.

God has appointed gifts in the assembly:
first emissaries,[a] second prophets, third
teachers, then miracle workers, healers,
helpers, administrators, and then those who
speak with various unknown languages.
1 Corinthians 12:28

Chapter 33

Only One could have predicted this.

At any given time, I am reading 3-5 books and 3-5 devotional plans on the Bible app.

So many books and never enough time!

I would periodically search infertility on the Bible app only to be disappointed and dismayed by the three lonely reading plans.

"I am going to submit my infertility group as a reading plan to the Bible app," I told Chad one night at dinner.

"Worth a shot," he replied.

He has to be used to my ambitious ideas by now, whether or not he actually thinks they are possible, I am not sure.

Although, I don't care.

Anything is possible, especially through Christ.

"There's only three, and I don't love them, so why not try?"

"Exactly."

It took me three months to find an email and actually have a human response. The Bible app had not been accepting submissions for a while. My frustrations finally came through in finding the right words to give them ears to hear me,

"I am Justine Froelker. I am a mental health therapist, infertility advocate, and bestselling author. National Infertility Awareness Week is coming up in April. I would like to submit a reading plan to help with your resources. Three reading plans for over 7 million people struggling with infertility is simply not enough. Our faith is one of the toughest pieces to hold on to through the difficult journey."

Magic words.

They allowed me to submit my plan and two weeks later it was published.

There is literally only one person who could have predicted that I, Justine Froelker, a pissed off, childless, doubter would ever have a published reading plan on the Bible app.

And, that is God himself.

Little did I know, I would end up having several.

Maybe, I am a Christian writer…

God – 34

Justine – 6

Who would have ever thought!

*Don't be mistaken; in and of ourselves
we know we have little to offer, but
any competence or value we have
comes from God.
2 Corinthians 3:5*

Chapter 34

"You love this baby fully in honor of the ones who made you a mother to begin with."

"Are you allowing yourself any excitement yet?" I ask my client who sits across from me. She is a relatively new client to me. She only called after being referred by a friend who also saw me through her own struggle. She is nine weeks pregnant after two losses. Naturally, she is really struggling with anxiety and worry.

"I can't, what if I lose this one too?" She says with tears filling her eyes. Her hands naturally move to her barely swollen belly, a belly that has both held and lost life twice before.

"Even if you try not to love this baby, I'm not sure it is possible," I say leaning forward in my chair towards her. "This baby deserves that love, and you deserve to be its mother."

"I don't think I will survive if we lose this one too."

"There is enough room for you to feel fearful and excited, to love and be realistic," I say. "Give yourself permission to feel both, because then it does not feel so impossible."

The tears begin to roll down her cheeks now, her guard drops and the sense of both emotions of anxious fear and loving excitement settle into her soul.

I continue, "Your children before this, although you may have never had the blessing to meet them, made you the mother you are today. You love this baby well because of them. You love this baby fully in honor of the ones who made you a mother to begin with."

"That sounds so hard."

"It is, and yet, it is what you and your babies deserve."

God – 35

Justine – 6

What a gift He has given me, and only through my three.

Instead, He brought you out of Egypt with overwhelming power and liberated you from slavery to Pharaoh the king because He loved you and was keeping the oath He swore to your ancestors.

Deuteronomy 7:8

Chapter 35

"I have to obey."

I only see her once every month or so, and there are times where I honestly have no idea what to expect when she walks into my office. Some months she is in a good place, doing the work and fighting through. Other weeks she is wanting to give up and not doing much to help herself. In the past, I have said to her, "We need you to stop creating fires. Do this work, this simple but not easy work of recovery, once and for all."

This week she walks in, and I cannot tell the space she's in.

"I came to something this week. I think I get it," she begins.

"What is that?"

"I have to obey," she says matter of factly.

"Obey?"

"Eventually I have to actually obey what you are recommending. I definitely have to obey how God wants me to live my life."

"I agree," I reply. "I also think there is a significant piece of surrender built into this work though too."

"Obey and surrender?"

"It is that Complicated Gray again. To hold both truths. I must obey what I know is required for this wholehearted and healthy life. My self-care, my own work, my faith. But I also, at the same time, have to surrender to what is not in my control. And, also to His plan."

"Damn this shit is hard."

"Simple, not easy, remember?"

God – 36

Justine – 6

Shit...obey.

Here is the patient endurance of the saints, those who keep the commandments of God and remain faithful to Jesus.
Revelation 14:12

Chapter 36

"I may, quite literally, be your worst nightmare come to life."

The alarm sounds much too early for a Saturday morning, especially after the work week I have had. It is the last day of National Infertility Awareness Week. I have maintained my two paying jobs while also working the *Ever Upward* job times ten during this week of raising awareness and pulling together my community.

I spent the week rallying my community on social media. Asking for stories and pictures of how we have not only survived but thrived through and after infertility and loss. After incredible support from my community on social media, my call for stories went viral, well viral for a story as hard as mine, and for this small time author with no assistant.

I had spent the week writing, sharing on social media and pushing out two incredible videos I made from everyone's words and pictures.

It was a fantastic week. One where I, for the first time, did not feel completely left out as the one who infertility treatments did not work.

But the week was not over, a few days ago my phone rang with an opportunity to speak to a room of a few hundred infertility patients. Months ago I was upset that I did not know about this opportunity and had to settle as a vendor instead of a speaker. And now, I had been asked to fill in for a last minute cancelation.

"Yes! You're okay with me speaking my messages?"

I said out loud on the phone

Oh my gosh, how am I going to pull this off. I am sooooo tired. But I will take that stage, and I will shine this light so bright, is what I was shouting inside.

Twenty minutes to share my story, my messages, to my ideal audience.

Thank you, God!

Finally!

"You look really great babe," Chad says as I finish up curling my overly bright red hair.

I had called the salon two days ago saying words I never thought I would say, "I have a hair emergency."

There was no way I was doing my first significant infertility speaking event with terrible gray roots!

"Thank you, do I look as exhausted as I feel?"

"Only because I know it," he jokes. "It will wear off once we get there.

My Mom tags along with us that morning to see me speak. We set up my books and business cards on the table and sit back to people watch with our coffee and my forbidden and oh so delicious donut. My stomach is churning already with nerves. I force a deep breath through my nose, hold for four and exhale through my mouth.

"Nervous?" Mom asks.

"I think I have to poop again," I reply, never one to shy away from authenticity.

"Better than throwing up I suppose."

Just as I draw another breath into my nose, a beautiful tall woman with dark hair approaches the table, "Justine?"

I stand up with my right hand reaching towards her, "Yes, I'm Justine Froelker."

"Hi, I'm Jen Myers from Y98…"

Holy crap, Jen Myers, from the freaking radio knows my name! She is the keynote speaker. Okay be true and be normal.

"I follow you on Twitter and had to meet you."

You had to meet me?

"Oh, hi! It is so nice to meet you," I reply. "Thank you so much for using your huge platform to continue to speak about your infertility journey and losses. We need voices like yours."

She shakes her head, "Thank you for the work you are doing."

We commiserate as two fellow warriors and survivors of the brutal journey of infertility and how difficult her PCOS diagnosis has been. "I'm looking forward to your keynote. I know it will be great."

"Thank you," she says as she walks away.

I sit down quickly next to Chad who is completely unaware of what just happened. He is used to having to tune out when people come up to me. Half the time they may be clients and the other half they are people who know me through the book. Either way, he assumes he is not welcome in the conversation, so he makes himself busy. What this also means is that he misses amazing stuff like this. "Well, that was amazing!"

"Who was that?"

With excitement, I recount everything he just missed, and like the incredible support he is, he is just as excited as I am.

"I may, quite literally, be your worst nightmare come to life. I am the woman who infertility treatments did not work. And yet, I know that I can help you not only survive but thrive through and after your journey. I think I may even be able to help it be more successful for you. Because I've dug my way out of the dark, I was made the mother I am to shine the light out for you."

Elephant in the room obliterated.

I finish up my talk with, "If you would like to have your book signed, please stop by my table. And, please reach out if you ever need support. Thank you so much for your time, your openness and kindness."

For my first real talk, I just nailed that.

My knees are shaking a bit still as I make my way to the bathroom. Just as I round my table to sit, I see a very distraught man making his way around my table. I stand to greet him. He is barely able to get the words out, "I just had to say thank you. You made me feel for the first time in three years. This has been so hard."

After him, another woman approaches my table, "Thank you for being the only person to get up today and say that sometimes this doesn't work and you can still be okay. Thank you for having the courage to speak anyway, we need to hear those stories too."

Then a couple, "Can we email you for some of those resources? We already downloaded a few that you mentioned."

Another woman, "Thank you for still speaking for us."

At first glance I may be the story that scares most people, I am the person who did not get what they wanted, hoped, prayed for, planned, and dreamed of. And yet, when I share my truth, the ugly and all, I am the story you also want.

Because I am okay.

I created a life of being better than okay, even after the worst case scenario happens.

God – 37

Justine – 6

Changing lives through the mother He made me.

Come to Me, all who are weary and burdened, and I will give you rest. 29 Put My yoke upon your shoulders—it might appear heavy at first, but it is perfectly fitted to your curves. Learn from Me, for I am gentle and humble of heart. When you are yoked to Me, your weary souls will find rest. 30 For My yoke is easy, and My burden is light.
Matthew 11:28-30

Chapter 37

"You're right; guys don't talk about their kids nonstop."

I sit at a table surrounded by five other women I've known for years but haven't seen in quite some time, especially all of us together. The wine flowed, except among the few who were pregnant, and a basket of forbidden (well, to me) gluten, with hand-whipped butter was being passed around the table.

I take a long sip of my red wine before taking the warm bread and smothering the butter onto it before taking a bite into a version of heaven to me.

I am here with no expectations, yet I am prepared to struggle a bit tonight with a few pregnant bellies and the only one at the table who is not a traditional mother. But it's been some time since I have seen everyone and even though it is not kids I have to share about, I still have an interesting life to share.

There is laughter, baby tips, and birth stories.

There is not one single inquiry for me.

Not one.

I feel invisible a lot, especially marketing a book about infertility and loss. I feel invisible in our society a lot as the woman who can't have kids, where many times I am quite literally the only one in just about every single place I go.

But I've never felt more invisible than at this dinner table despite being surrounded by old friends. I take a deep breath,

I engage in the conversation and clasp my hands beneath the tablecloth harder and harder as if the pressure between my hands will keep the tears from pouring down my face.

I say goodbye and hug them all with a smile on my face.

I click my seatbelt but skip turning on the radio like I usually do. I can't get out of the parking lot fast enough.

The first sob escapes as soon as I hit the highway.

By the time I get home, I am inconsolable.

I text one of my other Mom friends,

Thank you for seeing me, for always doing your best to make sure I don't feel invisible as the only one without kids. You have no idea how much that helps me survive this world.

Chad tries his best to console me as I try to contain myself, he says, "You can cry."

He can tell I feel stupid and frustrated but there was no holding in these kind of sobs, "It's not fair, you hardly ever have to deal with this."

He forced me into a hug and says, "You're right, guys don't talk about their kids nonstop."

He held me tighter and between sobs I managed to get out, "I will have to deal with this for the rest of my life."

As a therapist, hell as a human, I work hard to make sure every single person I am around feels seen, known and loved in my presence. Thriving after infertility without my own children has only strengthened this quality of mine.

Because I feel invisible almost all of the time, at least my shame shit storm stories tell me that.

I cannot contribute to sleep or feeding schedule banter.

Although I can share with you the current research on sleep hygiene and good self-care, which I'd argue will help a lot of parents.

I find myself constantly checking in with myself, is this about validation? One of my very first blog posts was about self-validation. How we must validate ourselves and not seek validation from anything or anyone else outside of us, most especially outside of His love and what Jesus did for us on the cross.

We are worthy.

We are enough.

Always.

And yet, being a woman without children means that quite literally I am the only one like me almost everywhere I go. It means I can be judged harshly for not having children, especially if they don't know the full story. It means frequently I am ignored. I don't have adorable kids to ooh and ahh over, and some may even say I am, therefore, not contributing to the future or society.

The holding of both truths of knowing I am okay, just me, and validating myself with the desire to be seen and known by others.

Perhaps it is just that, being seen and known cannot mean being validated.

Because I am responsible for my life, my wellbeing is in my hands, no one else's.

He gives us that free will, that choice to do the work to love ourselves, just as He loves us.

And, at the end of the day, especially, I am worthy because I am a child of the one true King. As my friend Caitlin says, "In the end, my identity does not come from hearing a child call me Mom but from knowing the King who calls me daughter."

God – 38
Justine – 6

In Him, through Him, and because of Him, I am enough.

But you are a chosen people, set aside to be a royal order of priests, a holy nation, God's own; so that you may proclaim the wondrous acts of the One who called you out of inky darkness into shimmering light.
1 Peter 2:9

Chapter 38

"Why don't you have kids?"

"That is really good art," Lane says as he is looking at my tattoos. "Did you draw them?"

"Aren't they beautiful? I didn't draw them. My friend did for me."

"She is very talented," he replies wisely beyond his years. "Why do you have them?"

"Because, buddy, sometimes grownups care about something a lot and they put it on their body because it is so important to them," I attempt to explain my meaningful but arguably obnoxious tattoos to my six-year-old, wise beyond his years, chosen child.

"They're pretty," he ends the conversation before turning to sit at the dinner table to eat.

At three he asked his Mom, "Why don't Justine and Chad have kids?"

His Mom replied with a generic, "Well, they have three dogs instead."

Tonight he asks in front of all of us at the dinner table, "Why don't you have kids?"

Before I can answer, his Mom says, "That's why they love spending so much time with you guys!"

It is a simple question from him, grounded in genuine loving curiosity. It is a loaded question for me that speaks volumes he is too little to understand yet. It is a question he deserves a truthful answer to, as it has to be confusing to see these people, who love him so much, not look like all the other families around him.

How do our friends answer this question in a way that honors their child's curiosity and respects the feelings and the story of us?

The answer is rarely simple.

Do they answer for us? Do they sugar coat? Do they change the subject? Are they fearful the truth is just too much for their children?

My answer, in honor of my truth and of the children I never got to hold in my arms, will always be with age-appropriate honesty: "We tried really hard to have kids but we can't. That is why we love seeing you guys so much."

"What do you mean you can't? Just keep trying."

"We had a lot of good doctors try to help us, but sometimes some people just aren't able to have their own kids."

"But what about kids who need parents?"

"We thought and prayed a lot about adoption, buddy, but for us, we decided it wasn't right for our family."

"But why?"

"Because every family is different, and we decided to fill our lives and give our love to all the awesome kids we have in our lives, like you!"

"So you love us a lot."

"Exactly, we love you guys a ton."

I suppose only time will tell how many times we will be asked this question by the many chosen children in our lives.

What I know for sure, is that they can always count on me for the truth.

God – 39

Justine – 6

A truth teller, safe landing spot, always seeing them non-Mom Mom.

My little children, don't just talk about love as an idea or a theory. Make it your true way of life, and live in the pattern of gracious love.
1 John 3:18

Chapter 39

The first group of daring women.

A woman flying in from New Jersey.

A woman driving all the way from Michigan.

A woman I've never met before.

Several of my clients.

All women who have dared to be brave enough to complete my day and a half Rising Strong™ intensive with me. It is work I never saw coming in my career and a calling I wasn't sure existed.

I'd like to think that everyone by now knows who Brené Brown is, yet our denial and unwillingness to practice vulnerability and talk shame tells me I know this is not true yet. Brené is a shame and vulnerability researcher with one of the most viewed TED talks of all time. I am blessed enough to be part of her team in that I am a Certified Daring Way™ Facilitator. Being a CDWF means I have the training and ongoing certification to do Brené's curriculum with my clients.

On a Friday night and Saturday, I will walk four women through the Rising Strong™ curriculum. We build community over yummy food, watch videos, share the stories we make up, dance, laugh and cry over the twelve hours we spend together doing the work.

Brené's work is all about living our lives bravely. Which means we will fail and fall and get our hearts broken. My Rising Ever Upward work is about how to learn from that fall and get up to love again.

It is the most powerful work of my 18-year career and my 38 years of life.

It is work I live out, practice, stumble through and practice again and again every single day of my life.

I teach it to my clients. I model it to my friends and family. And, I am declaring how much it can change the industry of network marketing, I've seen it on my own Plexus team.

What I could have never predicted was how powerful this work could be for others, as well as myself. God is always in that small group of four people, placing exactly who He needed there. He is also always there for me throughout the exhausting and exhilarating twelve hours of work.

Somewhere along the struggle, pain, loss, work, and triumph, He has gifted me this heartbreaking and brilliant story.

The story of a woman who can't have kids. The story of a woman who mothers more because of her three babies not here on earth with her. The story of a woman who defined her own happy ending. All to give others permission to struggle and to rise.

To shine the light for others to find, fight for, and create their second chance.

God – 40

Justine – 6

The gift of skills and new language to write our stories, and my usual potty mouth.

God rewrote the text of my life
when I opened the book of my heart
to his eyes.
Psalm 18:24 (The Message)

Chapter 40

"I will tell them my therapist says I have to rest."

"Did you eat Grandma?' I ask her as she is walking out of the hospital waiting room.

"Yes," she replies grabbing my arm and looking up at me with the most tired eyes I've ever seen.

"You need to sleep or at least rest some," I tell her with love.

"I will tell them my therapist says I have to rest," she says with a twinkle in her eyes.

Just an hour before this Chad's entire family stood at the bedside of his 88-year-old grandpa, as he passed from a stroke.

It was heartbreaking and peaceful.

It was the Complicated Gray.

Early that week, Chad had texted me from the hospital, "Waiting for someone to die is both morbid and peaceful, it is the epitome of the Complicated Gray."

Bossy has been used more than once to describe me. But I much preferred, Sheryl Sandberg's terminology, "She has executive leadership skills!"

I think since I don't have my own kids to mold, teach, and push the bossy Mom in me finds her outlets wherever she can.

My clients, my friends, my family, anyone.

I love teaching. I love pushing you to be a better version of yourself. I love loving.

I know the truth and importance of empathy. I've seen the power it all has when you take that empathy and wrap it with belief and resources.

That changes lives.

God – 41

Justine – 7

Stalemate – death is hard.

Please, Eternal One, don't hold back
Your kind ways from me.
I need Your strong love and truth
to stand watch over me and keep me
from harm.
Psalm 40:11

Chapter 41

"He welcomes them home."

I sit scrunched in the church pew by Chad's cousin in the second row. I have a decent view of Chad's grandma's profile, but I cannot see Chad at all on the other side of the church in the front pew. He is sitting with his cousins serving as a pallbearer.

We have all spent the last seven days together. The first several waiting for Chad's grandpa to pass after suffering a stroke from which he never awoke.

We were all together as Grandpa Biddie, took his last breath.

It was the ultimate Complicated Gray; loss, and peace.

The grief of losing a great man of 88 years, a husband of almost 68 years, a kind and faithful father, and the quiet and loving grandfather.

And, the peace of his passing, of no more pain or suffering, and being welcomed into the arms of his savior Jesus Christ.

Sitting in the pew next to Chad's cousin Jenny, both of us attempting to sing the right note alongside the organ player for the hymn and holding back sobs, I feel my eyes fill with tears.

Tears of grief and tears of peace.

Pastor Pam closes from the pulpit, "God never watches His children die. He welcomes them home."

Home to no pain and never feeling bad again.

Home to the glory of eternity.

I glance back over to look at Chad, and I can't help but think, home with our babies.

This brutal and beautiful life is all of it, all at once, and always.

The more I get to know this Complicated Gray, the discomfort and the permission of the space of holding two truths, the more enamored and grateful I am for it.

Friends, take a breath, look at your loved ones, feel your history, hope for your future and choose to love.

Life is hard. God is good.

And, it's all amazing.

God – 41

Justine – 7

Still hard.

My Father's home is designed to accommodate all of you. If there were not room for everyone, I would have told you that. I am going to make arrangements for your arrival. 3 I will be there to greet you personally and welcome you home, where we will be together. 4 You know where I am going and how to get there.

John 14:2-4

Chapter 42

Yep, that is me, one persistent mother.

It is baptism weekend, my favorite.

Four hundred people will walk into the waters of baptism, and I will eat yummy food truck food while listening to killer worship music in celebration.

In service that morning, sitting in our usual front row seats, Pastor Greg takes out a stack of papers to read several baptism applications, only a few sentences in and I know he is talking about me.

He says, "I finally went to the church in the cornfield to shut up my persistent therapist."

Yep, that's me, one persistent mother.

And, yes, I mean that to read both ways.

This client of mine has a story that takes you to your knees. In my 18 year career, there have only been a handful of clients who I have thought and even said out loud to them, "You have every reason in the world to stay sick and miserable. No one would even blame you. And, yet, there is absolutely no way you have been brought through that pain to suffer in the dark forever."

I pushed her, I mentored her, I worked harder than her at times, and I loved her well, especially and because the people in her life who were supposed to, did not.

I also sought lots of supervision on her.

That night at our church's baptism, I watched my client walk into the waters a new person; a person she has fought for and a person who did the wrestling work to finally give herself permission to accept His grace. A woman whose second chance at life is one I have always been able to see for her, but now with her faith, she can see for herself more clearly.

With my camera in hand and sweat trickling in places that should not sweat, my heart was full of pride, as she came out of those waters with more joy than I have ever seen.

Pride for her grit in this journey called life and pride in myself for having even the slightest bit to do with her walk into Christ's amazing grace.

God – 45

Justine – 8

We did that one together.

We are gardeners and field workers
laboring with God. You are the vineyard,
the garden, the house where God dwells.
1 Corinthians 3:9

Chapter 43

It is because of you I love harder and better.

To my three,

The three of you would have turned four this year.

Four.

The year of becoming little people. The terrible language barriers and potty training of the 2's out of the way and the dramatics of the 3's in our past.

Four.

The years I have spent wondering of you every day, feeling you always and wandering this earth with pieces of my soul tethered to heaven.

For quite some time, I've been told to write a letter to you. But, it wasn't until I asked one of my warrior mamas to write her babies a letter in hopes of her finding some clarity and healing, even within the uncertain darkness of infertility, that I realized you deserved and I needed my words.

I could write about how much I miss you and yet feel like I never had you. The weeks of synthetic hormones to retrieve you, the five days to only hear about your growth in a phone call from the infertility clinic and the gut-wrenching two weeks of praying and hoping you would stick in her warm uterus. All to end in a one-minute phone call with the words, "She's not pregnant." Years of trying, tens of thousands of dollars spent and lifelong dreams crushed in a phone call telling me our relationship was over before I even got to meet you.

I was not a mother.

And, I believed that for a long while.

It was dark. There were tears, a lot of anger, and a sense of self that disappeared behind never being seen.

I could write of all my wonderings. Would you have had my freckles or your Dad's blonde curls? Would you have been spunky like me or stoic like him? Would I have handled the poop and he the puke? What books would have been your favorite in your nighttime routine? What kind of grandparents would they have been? I could fill the biggest library on earth with my wonderings of the last four years, let alone of the lifetime of wonderings ahead of me.

I am a mother.

I worry, I wonder, I question, I doubt, I love.

Even if only from afar.

I could write how forgotten you and my motherhood are most days. No one speaks of you; some even say you don't count. Many aren't sure what to ask me or how to relate to me; a childless mother, I am often the only one everywhere I go.

The invisible mother.

The one without the happy ending.

Yet, only through you have I fought for, found, and created my own happy ending of thriving.

What I hope you know is how loved and wanted you were and are.

I hope I make you proud.

I hope every day you are honored in my work, my words, and especially, my love.

I have learned God gifted you to me, even if only for a whisper of time, as you were always His to begin with. I am blessed He chose me as your mother, it is the best gift I have ever received.

In the lifelong absence and the daily presence of you, I have found me.

It is because of you I notice every sunset and sunrise, see beauty in pain, feel with my whole being, believe in the unseen, give more than I ever have, seek the unknown, laugh with childlike wonder, walk with curiosity and have more gratitude for it all than ever before.

It is because of you I love harder and better.

It is because of you, I found Him.

Four.

I love you always.

Four.

Thank you, my loves.

Mom

God – 46

Justine -8

He made me a mother; they are nothing less than a miraculous gift.

Meanwhile, the Eternal One yearns to give
you grace and boundless compassion;
that's why He waits.
For the Eternal is a God of justice.
Those inclined toward Him, waiting for His
help, will find happiness.
Isaiah 30:18

Chapter 44

They would be proud.

"Is there a park nearby so we can get your last interview?" Ann, the director of *Don't Talk About the Baby*, a documentary about infertility and pregnancy loss that is featuring our story, asks.

"Yep, super close," I reply.

It was Saturday night, and we were both exhausted. We started filming my morning routine at sunrise and were approaching hour 14 of filming. We had spent the last two days filming no less than 12 hours.

We reached the park and stepped into the thick damp air of Saint Louis summer. Of course, there was a playground at the park. Of course, there was a little girl's birthday party. Of course, there were butterfly balloons at the party.

Of course.

I write this on August 31st.

It is August 31st again.

It comes every year.

They would be four this year.

Four years ago this day felt crushing. Four years ago that playground with a birthday party and butterfly balloons would have sent tears down my cheeks. Instead, I stood there while being filmed for a project that I wholeheartedly believe in and am honored to be a part of, taking it all in and giving myself permission to feel it.

The joy. The sadness. The pride. The longing.

The blessing and the manifestation.

It took me about a year to dig my way out of the darkness that was left after our failed infertility journey. A year of working with my therapist, building and wrestling with my faith, truly taking care of myself and re-engaging in my marriage. A year of owning all the parts of my story, speaking them, honoring my truth and my babies by creating this happy, healthy and magnificent version of myself.

Since then, all five of these years, I have spent working my butt off on making sure the infertility journey, hell life, does not leave us all empty shells of who we once were. Helping others to give themselves permission to feel it all, all at the same time; to feel the clarity and healing of the Complicated Gray. Writing and speaking the often ignored and rejected words of truth, the words to our freedom to ask for what we want and need and to have the courage to speak our truth always.

To shine the light of thriving out of the darkness to create our own second chances.

"I need you in every interview, this film is focusing a lot on you," Ann directed me at the beginning of our three days of filming.

"Oh, I didn't realize," I had replied.

I shook my head as if to clear the confusion. The confusion that after four years of rejection after rejection, being called terrible names on HuffPost, several negative reviews of *Ever*

Upward with the not so best of sales, being ignored by even some of my closest friends and family, money spent, the hardest and best work of my life for no pay, this was finally happening.

My truth and story, my healthy, although controversial, messages are the focus of a feature-length documentary on infertility and pregnancy loss. This was everything I had been working for.

There was no time to let it soak in, we had a movie to make, which I quickly learned was not for the weary.

Long hours, bug bites, lots of sweat, more wardrobe changes than you can imagine, pauses for planes and thunder and growling tummies all further complicated by my shock, disbelief, overwhelming gratitude, and relief that all of my work was paying off.

For three days straight for 12 to 15 hours a day, I was filmed while interviewing my friends, family, and clients. We discussed the heartache of infertility and pregnancy loss. We spoke our truths. We rallied the healthy messages of shattering the stigma and talking about our babies.

Just a few days later and after two mornings of letting myself sleep in, the fog and exhaustion of filming has lifted a bit. I've written some and processed the amazingness this all is, only to realize it is one of our due dates this day.

They would be four this year. And, this year I miss them, love them and wonder even more than the first three.

I am also more thankful for them than ever. They've helped make me who I am; a mother to many and a mother of second chances. It is because of them I am changing the world. I honor them with broken silence, hand holds in the power of *me too*, by embodying the warriorship of fighting for and creating a happy life in this world; a world without them and yet so much of them.

They would be proud.

They are my biggest blessings.

My life, a blessing through and because of them, is also a manifestation. A manifestation of my work and of my choices to embrace all the parts of my story and to always speak.

God made me the mother I am to do this work, to help others and to change the world.

I have done the work to create this incredible life and to be open enough to receive it. I have believed it was possible and that I am worthy of it. I have had the tenacity of every mother who loves and honors her children always.

It is a blessing made manifest.

And, it is only the beginning.

God – 47

Justine -8

Is this real life?

As a prisoner of the Lord, I urge you: Live a life that is worthy of the calling He has graciously extended to you.

Ephesians 4:1

Chapter 45

"I just got them back."

"Justine, you must listen to your own words," she says. "This is the Complicated Gray, and you must give yourself the grace to hold all the truths."

I am sitting in my crappy silver Sentra in a parking lot talking to my therapist Shellie for an emergency session.

The therapist having an emergency therapy session.

Fuck.

In all the years I have been seeing her or any therapist, I have never had an emergency session. But, last night my parents sat Chad and me down and dropped what felt like a bomb. They are unhappy in Saint Louis and have decided to move back home to Iowa.

Shellie continues, "What are you feeling and thinking?"

"I obviously, more than anything, want them to be happy. But we do not agree with this decision at all, I don't think home is healthy for them, and I think this decision is rash and that they have not given it a fair shot here. Then there is the ego part of me. That everyone back home will be thinking, told you so, they should have never moved away. Then there is the hurt and rejected daughter part of me. And, well, she is utterly heartbroken."

My voice catches.

"You're hurt and maybe even feeling rejected."

"I am never enough for my family, ever," I say through tears. "Plus, I just got them back."

The rational part of my brain knows that this decision is nothing personal and is not meant to hurt me at all. Yet, it literally breaks my heart. I left home for college when I was 18, having Mom and Dad near me felt like it was finally my time to enjoy them.

And, of course, shame and scarcity weren't too far behind.

If I had kids, you wouldn't be leaving.

The surprised, caught off guard, and hurt daughter actually said that to them last night.

Shit. Shame and trauma have some bitch ass claws.

"Justine, you quite literally did your job too well," Shellie interrupts my thoughts and tears. "You rehabbed them. They have never been healthier in their lives. So now they want to go home."

The work of this *Ever Upward* journey, especially in the mess of the Complicated Gray, means holding both truths in difficult times with the people you love most.

I am so hurt and disappointed, and I will forgive you.

Uncomfortable, and downright pisses me off some days.

"But this was supposed to be their home."

God – 47

Justine – 9

A faithful broken heart is still a broken heart.

Eternal One: *My intentions are not always yours,*
and I do not go about things as you do.
My thoughts and My ways are above and beyond you,
just as heaven is far from your reach here on earth.
Isaiah 55:8-9

Chapter 46

Until I see her.

I work on my phone on the twenty-minute drive to church. There are two months a year I am very busy as an infertility and loss thriver and advocate: April (National Infertility Awareness Month) and October (National Pregnancy and Infant Loss Awareness Month). I feel the car slow and glance up to notice the string of cars with brake lights illuminated as far as we can see.

Pumpkin patch.

Damn pumpkin patch (at least for this woman who can't have babies).

It is that time of year that every week on our way to church we will pass the biggest and most popular pumpkin patch in Saint Louis. I will look to my right every single week for about six weeks and see the orange pumpkins of every size with children crawling all over them while their parents try to get the annual picture.

A reminder, again, that I will never have that experience with my own children.

This Sunday is different though as I work on finding and saving pictures about pregnancy and infant loss on my phone to share each day of the month. It is different because of what I know is waiting for me in the service this week in church. I sigh and look over at Chad just as the traffic begins to pick back up to normal pace, "This is literally an infertile woman's road of hell. Passing the pumpkin patch full of kids at a slow pace as if to rub it in even more while on the way to child dedication day at church."

He half-laughs with a sigh. I know he both gets it and doesn't.

We walk into the enormous auditorium just as the first song plays. This is late for us, we are usually here early and have our butts planted in our front row center seats at least ten minutes before the service starts. I knew this week I would not want to be in those seats.

Front row center to the dream that will never be yours...no thank you.

The usher sees us trying to find a seat and motions us to our right, and I immediately notice the chairs are marked "family section." I shake my head and feel my heart rate rise as I make eye contact with Chad. The usher motions again to the same section. I start to feel the panic rise inside of me, *Seriously God?*

I look at Chad and try to get him to hear me when I says, "I am not sitting in the family section on child dedication day."

He makes the connection and follows me as I bolt to the opposite side of the auditorium, and we finally find seats in the upper part of the auditorium.

The music swells, and we are taken to church, just like every Sunday. After one song the lights come up, and I see the families being led to the front of the stage with their babies.

Here we go.

Chad puts his hand on my leg, and I clasped my hands tightly together as if the pressure will keep the tears in this year. My own grief is a tiny bit subdued this year because we have two sets of friends at the front with their adorable daughters. I am able to focus on them for the most part which means my own longing awakens inside of me just a bit.

Until I see her.

I can only see her orange shirt, and her dark hair pulled into a ponytail and how tightly her husband is holding her. Her husband's arm is wrapped around her, and I know it is serving multiple purposes, to both hold her up and to love her. She wipes tears from her face the entire ten minutes that our pastor talks about us as a congregation supporting and loving these families and these children in their walk with Christ.

My own tears escape the rims of my eyes to fall onto my cheeks. Chad puts his arm around me for only a second knowing that if he lingers too long, I will lose it myself.

The music swells up. I see her take a deep breath just as her husband's fingers interlace with hers behind her back.

She wipes more tears.

I wipe my own.

I see her.

I am her.

I only wish there had been an open seat next to her because I would have gone down to sit beside her and grab her hand while we both allowed tears to flow down our cheeks.

Last year at child dedication I was overcome by breath stealing sobs. So much so, I had to sit down in the dark during the song to try to calm myself.

The thoughts and feelings that go through a woman struggling with any version of the infertility or loss story during a child dedication run the gamut:

Why them and not me?

Will I ever be a mother?

I will never be up there.

I am supposed to be up there this year.

I wonder if those twins are from IVF?

They seem older, and I bet they had to do treatments.

My parents will never get to experience this joy.

God, have you forgotten me?

They would have been four this year.

Why do they never mention couples like us...

I am a mother too...

This year right after the dedication they played Christ is Enough.

As a believer, I know this and trust it.

As a forever longing Mom, my aching heart can sometimes doubt it.

My breath catches as we sing:

Through every storm

My soul will sing...

The cross before me

The world behind me

More than ever these words are true for me.

They are true, and I still long for my babies.

I wonder.

I love.

I weep.

I love even harder and more.

It is with this forever scarred and always healing soul and my heart full of longing joy that I want to say to the invisible mom crying in church,

You are not alone. Even though it feels as if you are invisible like no one remembers us or cares enough to see us, you are not invisible.

I see you. I know you. I am you. We are mothers too.

God – 47

Justine -10

Mothers like us matter too, especially in His eyes.
Ugh, get with it churches.
Has the score made it pretty obvious,
I am on the struggle bus.

So don't be afraid. I am here, with you;
don't be dismayed, for I am your God.
I will strengthen you, help you.
I am here with My right hand to make right
and to hold you up.
Isaiah 41:10

Chapter 47

*A holiday card of three Christmas jammied tortured
little dogs.*

"You ready?" my parents ask me.

"I have to get a picture of the Glasswing butterfly first," I reply. "Chad saw it a few minutes ago."

The butterfly aviary is one we are familiar with, as we visit it every single year we go to Branson. In fact, it was a year ago that I met Julie who then sent me information on the Glasswing butterfly after reading my blog.

The Glasswing, as well, as the monarch, are my mascots.

Spirit animals? Whatever, their existence helps me to survive my own.

The air is colder than usual in the aviary and not as humid as it usually is, which also means the butterflies are not as active that day. We had already had a huge surprise when we first got there when I spotted my coloring journal *Taking Flight*. I had completely forgotten they sold it there in the gift shop.

I love butterfly houses, but I also knew I needed pictures to use for my online writing and social media, so it was both work and pleasure, the always delicate balance of my life. I had all but forgotten about the Glasswing until Chad finally spotted it a few minutes prior.

Every single time I get close enough for a shot her transparent wings and tiny body become a blurred flit in the air challenging our eyes to keep track of her. Her frantic movement remind me of my life those last several weeks. I had been busy, busier than I had ever been. Yet, I also tried to stop referring to it as busy because that can become such an excuse for so many of us.

I'm too busy, has become like nails on a chalkboard for me

It is a fact; we are all busy. Life will never get unbusy.

We must choose our busy.

Much like the Glasswing butterfly, most days I feel like a crazed flit in the air that no one can catch.

There was a difference though; this butterfly lived in a home decked with Christmas joy of music and decorations. I, on the other hand, have yet to put up a single snowman or glitter garland this year. Christmas is less than 20 days away, and I didn't have one bit of Christmas jolly in my house. My excuse had been my crazed business and being out of town so much.

Or so I thought.

Then, the day before, on a gray and chilly Saint Louis morning God stopped me in my tracks. As my gigantic-never-gets-all-the-way-done to-do list ran through my head, I caught a glimpse of movement in the backyard. At first, it was only the whites of their tails that caught my eye against our tree line that had gone mostly brown.

Three deer were standing in a row.

Three.

My three.

They all stopped to look at me in their statue-like grace as I stepped onto a chair to get a better view of them through our back windows. I found myself taking a deep breath; a paused, deep breath in spite of my looming to-do list and every passing minute that nothing is getting crossed off of it.

My chosen busy lately had been a ton of amazing travel, continuing to see a full-time caseload of clients (including doing more Rising Ever Upward intensives, which I love), working on the second (this) book proposal and building my Plexus team, my network marketing side gig.

It is all stuff I absolutely love and wholeheartedly believe in.

It is on top of that chair seeing God's not so gentle reminder of my three, that I realized I had also been busy because I am passing through another damn holiday and looming due date without my three.

We were "supposed" to have four-year-olds that Christmas. Four-year-olds in their matching Christmas jammies giggling with magical excitement as they leave a note, cookies, and milk for Santa and sprinkle glitter on our front yard for the reindeer.

Instead, I tortured our three little dogs with their own Christmas jammies for that year's holiday card.

I got the shot of the Glasswing butterfly because I am one determined woman running three businesses with the frenzied grace just like that of a Glasswing butterfly.

I still haven't crossed everything off that damn to-do list, and probably never will. I will keep on in this wholehearted hustle knowing I am always enough (or at least I'm going to keep telling myself that).

With God's gentle reminder, I will stop and feel the forever longing joy. I know better than to think I can busy myself enough to forget about the grief of my life.

They would have been four.

I miss them and wonder always.

I am thankful *and* I am sad.

The holidays only make all of the feels, all the more palpable, no matter how long that to-do list is.

Be still my child, He must constantly remind me.

You see, God also gave me Chad. The night before we left for Branson, after dinner out with friends I walked into the house to see an oddly shaped, delicious smelling and plain as day Christmas tree. "You said you wanted a real one," Chad had said with love in his eyes.

My eyes filled with tears, "I did."

He looks back at me with confusion, as to him, it is only a tree and a nice gesture for his wife.

To me, it is a tree that reminds me that my house is missing a few four-year-olds to help me decorate it, and so it is also one more thing on that never-ending to-do list.

I am finding you never quite know how grief will hit you year to year, especially with the holidays or special dates. What I do know is that we cannot busy ourselves enough to forget about it.

It is a huge part of us, and always will be. I am honored and grateful to be their mother, all within my forever longing for them.

So I guess the question really is: How long will the tree stay bare?

Not as long as my heart will ache.

God –48

Justine –11

He's there, I am listening, and grief is brutal.

Eternal One: Don't revel only in the past,
or spend all your time recounting the victo-
ries of days gone by.
Watch closely: I am preparing something
new; it's happening now, even as I speak,
and you're about to see it. I am preparing
a way through the desert;
Waters will flow where there had been none.
Isaiah 43:18-19

Chapter 48

"Why are you still struggling so much?"

The lights cast a glow throughout the house that is both calming and unnerving.

The scent of pine brings both joy and sadness.

The stubborn ache in my chest like a constant reminder of what could have been and the gift of what is.

December was kicking my ass the year they were to turn four.

I was tearful easily. I was overwhelmed with it all.

And, I know I am not alone.

Most people, even my closest loved ones, are asking, "But, why are you struggling so much?"

Side note: This is not the most empathetic way to asks.

Then there were my fellow warriors and even my always trying husband, who are asking with empathy and love, "Is this different or harder than last year? How come you think you're struggling so much?"

I am as surprised (and annoyed honestly) as anyone else, as I would like to say, and think and experience, that this gets easier.

Every year that passes there is this naive part of you that thinks it won't hurt as bad. Maybe, just maybe, it will get better. But as I always say, it just gets different.

There is a myriad of reasons that Christmas season is kicking my butt. Bottom line, infertility and loss change you forever. If we choose to do the work it changes us for the better, I promise. No amount of twinkling lights, carols, jingle bells and damn glitter (literally, damn glitter, it should not be allowed on cards in my opinion) lessens the longing in my soul that comes from wishing my three were here with me on earth. In fact, those lights, carols, bells, and glitter only remind me of everything I do not get with my own children. They remind me of what I am missing out on and of what is missing of me.

Admittedly, all that missing out and grief stir up the voice in my head and the ache in my heart that tells me I am not enough, that I will never be enough, especially because I am not a mother.

Yet, I have done the work, and I know this is not my truth.

And still, shame weasels in so quickly and steals my light.

I have changed that story...most days. Through the work I have done, and especially in my faith I know my truth is that I am worthy, I am enough, *and* I am a mother.

This year of them turning four seems like my shitty first draft, as we say in the Rising Ever Upward curriculum, of *I am not enough* wins more days than not.

One Sunday on the live stream of my church service, I desperately took notes and attempted to control my tears. I had two friends who were watching, text me to see if I was okay.

As soon as we sang *O Holy Night* with the lyric, *and the soul felt its worth*, a peace settled into my soul right next to my forever longing.

***Be still, my child. It is Me, AND it is about Me. I am here
with you always.***

My worth is not in children by my side, in being called Mom
or being seen as someone who matters by society. My worth is
in Him and what better time of year than now to remember that.

God didn't promise me a baby. He promised He would
always be there.

Deep Complicated Gray breath.

I still never fully decorated our tree or put up any other
Christmas decorations, and I am giving myself permission that
it is okay.

This hurts, and it always will. I am sad, and that is okay. I
may feel invisible, and I am worthy.

These are my truths.

And, so I look through the glow of the unadorned lit tree
filling my lungs with the scent of pine in a deep knowing breath,
to feel the ache and the awe, the longing and the joy, my worth,
His love and my three.

God – 49
Justine -11

There is room for it all.

*So also you have sorrow now, but I will see
you again, and your hearts will rejoice, and
no one will take your joy from you.*
John 16:22 (English Standard Version)

Chapter 49

Yes, I am that kind of Christian.

Five years ago, the year they were to be four, it was Christmas time that we were in our first, and what we thought would be our only, two-week wait.

I only did the math because Facebook reminded me via the *On This Day* reminder the other day, as five years ago I posted a vague post about the two-week wait.

Then I posted nothing else about it... It seems my brave-speak-the-truth advocacy did not develop until after our infertility journey ended and I fought my way out of my fetal position to rise from the ashes.

That year, I remember we went home to Iowa for Christmas showing off black and white pictures of bubble globs to all our family; those globs being our eight-celled embryo babies.

The babies we never got to meet. We were confident it had worked. It had to work, as it was our only chance.

That only chance was crushed with a one-minute phone call followed by me trying not to throw up in the trash can and Chad literally holding his tears in as I completely lost it.

We took the loan out the next day for another try. That one didn't work either.

As timing would have it our infertility anniversary dates, exist alongside our due date, and oh yea, Christmas season.

Infertility clinics really should note the timing of these things. Every December I am haunted by dates that will be forever seared into my heart and soul.

Dates that are sad and dates that made me a mother.

Once again, I am reminded of my work by a decent smack upside the head, as He often likes to work with me. The work to embrace the Complicated Gray, and to choose the joy within this sadness, as there is always room for both.

In the midst of many desperate-on-my-knee prayers during this week, I realize and am reminded of how strongly we can feel two "opposing" emotions at the same time.

- I am forever longing and sad and also grateful for the mother He made me, even if they aren't here with me– *longing joy.*

- I love my life and how much I have worked to thrive after loss, and I miss my three more than words can says–*grateful guilt.*

This is the hard ass work of walking in the freeing truth of the Complicated Gray.

And, the more I think about it and learn, we are nowhere near the first to walk this walk. Perhaps, we had a model who did it best a long, long time ago.

Jesus longed *and* loved. He angered *and* loved. He grieved *and* loved. He struggled *and* He trusted His Father,

...*not my will, but yours be done.*

Luke 22:42

And yes, I am that kind of Christian, I just wrote ass and quoted Jesus all within a few lines.

He knows me. He sees me. He understands me.

This faith and truth do not make the Complicated Gray easier to feel and muster through. It does, however, ground me and help me to stand my sacred truth. That even though I shake my fist at Him on some days because the story He has written for me hurts like hell, makes me sad and feels unfair, I know and trust that He's got this, that He knows me, knows me best, and knows what is best, and that He has my ending.

He is my perfect loving Father.

My only job is to emulate His love, walk in my truth and to choose joy.

Because when I do that, I honor my three and myself.

And, that my friends, is the best thing any mother can do for herself and her children.

God – 50

Justine -11

He walked it first, even the messy, muck of the Complicated Gray.

The Voice took on flesh and became human and chose to live alongside us. We have seen Him, enveloped in undeniable splendor—the one true Son of the Father—evidenced in the perfect balance of grace and truth.

John 1:14

Chapter 50

Shit and yes!

"Would you be willing to tell a little of your story on stage?"
Pastor Jake emailed. Chad and I are facilitating another semester
of QuarterLife and Jake is working hard to change things up
because allowing the space required for 20-somethings to turn
towards and walk with Christ is not a feat for the weak spirited
or uncreative.

"Of course, what are you thinking?" I quickly reply to
Jake's email.

"I am going to have three of you share your story, one about
the uncertainty and anxiousness of life, one about the struggle
after super hard stuff, and then one about basically making the
best of it, that's who I want you to be," Jake emailed back.

Yep, that's me, making it a gift. Sarcasm and truth here!

Sitting on stage I couldn't control my voice from shaking,
telling my story is one thing, coming from it with Christ is still
kind of new to me. Over one hundred 20-somethings looked
at me as I walked them through the briefest version of my
story: 2 back surgeries, a year in a body cast, tried to have
babies, and can't. You could see their discomfort and awe in
their expressions.

As I pause, Jake asks, "Can you tell us how you turned
towards Christ or prayed? How'd you get here?"

"It was an ugly and mighty faith wrestle there for a while. And, then I gave myself permission to just talk to God. He knew I was angry, and He is big enough to handle that. So I talked to Him. I also gave myself permission to know that even on those hard days, the ones I shake my fist at Him and curse the story He has written for me, and I assure you there will be those days for the rest of my life. Even on those days, I can trust the story He has written for me and know he has the ending."

After I spoke, I had a young man approach me to thank me for my courage and for my story. He says, "My wife died a year ago, thank you for giving me permission and for reminding me that God is big enough and already knows how I feel. I can just talk to Him."

"Yes! And, then maybe we can actually heal, right?"

Two people, vastly different lives and losses, sitting beside with one another with their struggles and pain, bearing witness and honoring their truths.

God – 51

Justine -11

Whew, loss, it's just loss, it's all loss, fuck, its loss.

You even know the small details like when I
take a seat and when I stand up again.
Even when I am far away, You know what
I'm thinking.
Psalm 139:2

Chapter 51

"It gets different."

My mourning grew quiet, my feet rose to dance.

We are in the front row of church with the music washing over my entire body and seeping into my heart. I catch the tears before they hit my cheeks when this line comes onto the screen and is sung with such clarity to me that my next breath catches in my throat.

Over the last five years since ending infertility treatments without the desired, prayed for, planned for, hoped for and paid for, healthy babies in my arms, my mourning has had its own journey. As I allow these words to settle into my forever scarred soul, I feel a sense of peace. A peace that I am not sure I have ever felt before.

My mourning will never go away.

Remember, it doesn't get better, it gets different.

And yet, there are beginning to be more and more days where my mourning has grown quiet.

Better yet, it has grown quiet enough for me to rise and dance.

Never an easy task.

One that does not come without a plethora of mixed emotions either.

And still, it is a rising dance.

A rising out of the darkness and into the gray of life.

Because when I rise, better yet, when I rise to dance, I am awake.

I am awake to all that life, and God has to offer me, heartbreak and all.

Awake to this brilliant life full of soul filling color.

God –52

Justine -12

We're dancing together.

*Eternal One: Young women will
dance for joy;
young men will join them, old ones too.
For I will turn their mourning into joy.
I will comfort My people and replace their
sorrow with gladness.*
Jeremiah 31:13

Chapter 52

Hello Lindsay, want to be my infertility best friend?

The email reads, "First, I found your site before I realized you were from Saint Louis and then I "squeeeeeeeled" a lot afterward. I too am a Saint Louisian, an author, and blogger, and I love the work of Brené Brown (though I'm not a facilitator)." She goes on to share some of her own infertility story and to share her new self-care during the two-week wait book. And, then she asks me to lunch!

Wait, I am not the only self-published author writing about topics no one wants to talk about? Yes, please, can we have wine too? Hello Lindsay, want to be my infertility best friend?

We become immediate friends–a story so different and so much the same, both in infertility and in who we are as humans, her radiant smile with dimples for days, and her beautiful arm tattoo. We could have talked for hours.

She is embarking on her first round of IVF, and I am years out of our journey without the kids. Many would say we couldn't be friends. Many would choose to hold on to their pain so tightly that a friendship, let alone one with as much safe honesty as ours has, would never be a possibility.

Instead, we give one another permission to struggle and to rise, together.

It didn't hurt that we had many of the same frustrations with our own community. The comparisons of journeys, especially in numbers.

"I've done four rounds of IVF."

"Well, I've done 10."

The bitterness, anger, and trauma that so many are struggling to work through. The never, ever, ever give up message that is killing marriages, bank accounts, bodies, and souls.

We just get one another.

And, then we got to go on stage together and teach.

And, it was magic.

I cannot wait to see where our journey takes us. All we know, hope, and I pray for, is that we will be plus two at the end of 2017. Because we both also know how much infertility steals from us. We've heard and seen the worst case scenario happen over and over, some of us are the worst case scenarios. Until she has her healthy twins in her arms, it is hard to take a deep breath.

I can't wait to meet them.

And, I can't wait to change the world with their Mom.

God – 53

Justine – 12

I'm not completely alone, the only one speaking these messages.

Two are better than one because a good return comes when two work together. 10 If one of them falls, the other can help him up. But who will help the pitiful person who falls down alone?

Ecclesiastes 4:9-10

Chapter 53

She's a bit woo woo for my taste.

"I think I am done with therapy for now," I say to Chad over the dinner table with a hint of questioning in my voice that at least I can detect and feel.

"I could have told you that a while ago," he replies. "What happened today in session?"

"She just doesn't give me much in return, and in reality, it is because I have already worked through it."

"What are you thinking?"

"It's time for a coach, for sure."

"I could have told you that a while ago, too."

Thanks, Chad.

Several months before this conversation I had gone through a virtual coaching program with Jen Sincero, author of *You Are a Badass*.

Awesome book, get it.

It is incredible.

And, the best part was being part of a Facebook community with 600 other like-minded, badass people. This made it easy to know exactly who I wanted to reach out to for personal coaching first.

I had actually emailed Cassandra months prior when I was knowingly struggling, and after a few messages, I felt like she basically told me I wasn't ready for her.

She was right.

And, it wouldn't be the first time.

After a great consultation phone call, I took a deep breath, paid her high, and much deserved, fee and officially became a therapist with a coach.

We're still working together.

Never more in my life have I had someone push me, educate me, pump me up, be more excited for me, and accept me for who I am while also seeing who I have the power to be.

She's a bit woo woo for my taste, and she has gotten me to listen to and read some pretty weird stuff since working with her. She allows me to bring Christ into my work because it just isn't an option not to. And, together it is some crazy amazing co-creating.

Yep, I love Jesus, and curse words, a little too much, I promise I am working on it it, and I know the power of all that woo woo weirdo affirmation and manifestation shit, because guess what? Jesus did it first.

Our work together is changing everything. I've changed my relationship with my pain, I have manifested some of my biggest dreams, and taken the most significant risk of my entire life.

Those are all stories for the next book.

And, it is all just the beginning.

God – 54
Justine –14

Woo woo and Christ make for one helluva team.

Jesus: 22 Trust in God. 23 If you do, honestly, you can say to this mountain, "Mountain, uproot yourself and throw yourself into the sea." If you don't doubt, but trust that what you say will take place, then it will happen. 24 So listen to what I'm saying: Whatever you pray for or ask from God, believe that you'll receive it and you will.
Mark 11:22-24

Chapter 54

Do you want to be a therapist?

We are probably about half-way through our first coaching contract when Cassandra asks several times and in several ways, "Do you want to see clients anymore?"

I would always hem and haw, "I can't imagine not seeing clients. I mean, that is who I am: I am a therapist...and, I want more."

Who is this mother without her kids?

"Can it look different?" she asks.

"I don't even know how" I reply. "What I do know, is that I want to reach more people. I love the teaching piece and the coaching. I LOVE my workshops and intensives. There are sessions that it feels like it is a waste of my talents, which sounds soooo bad."

"It's time to widen your scope."

It was within a matter of three calls that all of a sudden, I was headed on tour...an eight-city tour to be exact, offering my workshops and intensives based on Brené Brown's work. I'd been doing my own small group intensives for a year with great success and amazing results. Between my audiences with my books and my Plexus business, it was time to bring the work to the people.

So, we planned. We marketed. We educated, and I basically closed my practice for the entire summer.

Tour has been one of the hardest and most amazing things I have ever done.

Surely, God hasn't brought me to this only to fail?

God – 55

Justine –15

Tied again, man it is hard to trust struggle and change in the moment!

Be strong, courageous, and effective. Do not fear or be dismayed. I know that the Eternal God, who is my God, is with you. He will not abandon you or forsake you until you have finished all the work for the temple of the Eternal.
1 Chronicles 28:20

Chapter 55

Take this cup. Not my will.

"I can't stop listening to chapter 8 where she talks about Jesus being the ultimate example of surrender and co-creation," I tell Cassandra on our call that day.

"What is it that is blowing your mind?" Cassandra asks.

"It is the freaking Complicated Gray!" I frustratingly and kind of yell back at her.

She waits for me to continue.

"I mean what happens in that space between the, *take this cup*, and the, *your will, not mine*? I want to know more! How was Jesus feeling? What was he thinking? How much time passed between those statements? I mean, I have poured over them in the gospels, and it is like literally just two statements back to back."

Cassandra lets me asks the questions, and we talk a bit more, but she knew I would need to talk to some of my pastors at church about this concept.

After lots of googling questions and more reading, I feel even more frustrated than clear.

Am I really the only one that is wondering what Jesus felt and thought in that moment?

What I have concluded thus far is that we don't know how much time passed between those two statements, and we will probably never know for sure what Jesus was thinking or feeling.

Just as He was all divine and all man, he was also all surrender and choice.

He walked it first.

He was the Complicated Gray.

Perhaps, it is in this space, that we can also give ourselves permission to be all, to think all, to feel all, *and* all at the same time.

This, I believe, and I have found, is where our magic, our clarity, and our healing lie…right in the middle of the Complicated Gray.

And, of course, He is right there with us.

God – —

Justine – —

Don't think we need that score anymore, do you?

Jesus: *Father, if You are willing, take this cup away from Me. Yet not My will, but Your will, be done. Luke 22:42*

Though He was in the form of God,
He chose not to cling to
equality with God;
7 But He poured Himself out to fill a
vessel brand new;
a servant in form
and a man indeed.
The very likeness of humanity,
8 He humbled Himself,
obedient to death—
a merciless death on the cross!
Philippians 2:6-8

Chapter 56

Will you walk in this muck with me?

It has been five years since we ended our infertility journey, I still wonder every day who my three would have been.

What I don't wonder anymore, is who I would be.

I am a forever grieving mother, and I am a woman who chooses to do the work to consider it pure joy and to make it all a gift.

It is messy. It is super hard. On some days, it can even get real ugly.

It is a wonder-filled life where I belong, and a life more beautiful than I ever dreamed or imagined.

Will you walk in this muck with me?

Are you willing to grab your brave, give yourself permission, and embrace all the parts of your story? All the feels? All at once?

We can do it together.

Walking alongside and sitting beside one another in this life with our struggles and most especially our risings.

Because, when we do, we can heal a little more, and together, we can finally begin to thrive in the darkness of grief and live our lives freely, with the permission of The And.

Consider it pure joy, my brothers and sisters,[a] whenever you face trials of many kinds, 3 because you know that the testing of your faith produces perseverance. 4 Let perseverance finish its work so that you may be mature and complete, not lacking anything.
James 1:2-4 (New International Version)

Epilogue

The mother of second chances.

I reach over to set my journal on my nightstand and grab my latest nighttime reading of choice. I hear the Sonicare toothbrush Chad was using in the bathroom as he gets ready for bed. Our nighttime routines were so different: his is of basic hygiene and mine is of basic sanity.

I read for just five to ten minutes before I know it was getting too late, or until my eyes wore out, whichever comes first. I set my book on my nightstand on the pile of my devotionals, along with my journal, which is also next to the pile of other books. As I twist to turn off the light, I hit the journal, and everything topples to the ground.

"How many of these books have you read?" Chad asks as he peeks out of the bathroom.

"I haven't bought new ones in forever. I promise, I am using the library," I say getting defensive right away.

"I didn't say anything about that," he answers back with no defensiveness and in his Chad calm.

"Sorry, um, maybe half," I reply.

"Can you sell the half you have read?"

"Good idea," his business-like mind is always at work and almost always right.

I am a seeker and a constant learner. At any given time, I am reading three books and have no less than 20 tabs open on my phone and computer, each, of articles and videos I want to read or watch.

I am a plethora of resources for my clients and my loved ones, whether or not you want them, I will tell you about them.

Bring a journal when we go to lunch because you will take notes.

I love learning. I love trying new things.

How will we ever know if something can help us if we never give it a try?

It's how I dug my way out of the dark after our failed infertility journey. Trying weird things, albeit backed by research like Alpha-Stim, adult coloring books, and meditation.

It's how I have continued to define my own happy ending… by creating this second chance life…by writing what I want to write, and writing it no matter if anyone reads it or whether or not it will ever actually pay a bill or create one.

It's how I started another business, although this time, one that I never, ever thought I would do: network marketing.

Cue the dramatic dun, dun, dunnnnn.

I created my own second chance life in my daily choices, and in this life, I have figured out 'what makes my heart sing', as Carmine Gallo writes in *Talk Like Ted*.

I love myself in the action of my self-care, because Jesus walked it all first providing me with an incredible example.

Because I am worthy of a fully life, the life He created me for.

I am the mother of second chances.

My gift, the gift of the three babies I never got to hold in my arms, the babies who were always His to begin with, is that they made me a mother.

And, they brought me to Him.

It has been in the most significant loss of my life that I fought for, created, and received the life He gave His for.

I want to help you see, create, and fight for your second chance in life too.

I am a mother of second chances…and I will teach you to be the same.

Acknowledgements

To you, the reader, especially if you have made it this far, thank you. The time and heart space it takes to finish a book is something I do not take lightly. Thank you for joining me.

To my community who has waited so long for this project, thank you for your patience, your encouragement, your love, and most of all for showing up for yourself throughout these few years as I share my gifts, my struggles, and my stories with you.

To my parents, thank you for allowing me to seek and change, thank you for loving me through it always, and thank you for letting me share my faith and my Jesus with you.

To my church, The Crossing and all the pastors and staff there, thank you for providing the safe space for me to ask the hard questions, to wrestle, and most of all, thank you for allowing me and my story to be a part of what God is doing there.

To my friends, especially those who read through this book two years after it was written after much difficulty through the editing process. Your time, your feedback, your love, and most of all your belief in me and this project is something I am forever grateful for and the biggest reason I didn't scrap this entire book to begin with.

To Chad, my witness and my solid foundation of sanity, love, laughter, and true partnership in this life, thank you for your belief in me, thank you for your patience as I fought my way to Jesus, and thank you for loving me the way you do.

To my three, thank you for choosing me as your mother.

To my loving Father, thank you for the gift of my three, thank you for finding me in the darkness of my anger, and thank you for being there, loving me, and knowing me the entire time, even if I wasn't ready to receive it.

CPSIA information can be obtained
at www.ICGtesting.com
Printed in the USA
LVHW030615220221
679516LV00002B/139

9 781545 650455